50 Heart-Healthy Food Recipes for Home

By: Kelly Johnson

Table of Contents

- Grilled Salmon with Lemon and Dill
- Quinoa-Stuffed Bell Peppers
- Mediterranean Chickpea Salad
- Baked Chicken with Herbs
- Spinach and Kale Smoothie
- Lentil Soup with Vegetables
- Whole Wheat Pasta Primavera
- Grilled Vegetable Skewers
- Avocado and Black Bean Salad
- Turkey and Vegetable Stir-Fry
- Roasted Garlic and White Bean Dip
- Cauliflower Rice Stir-Fry
- Greek Yogurt Parfait with Berries
- Tuna and White Bean Salad
- Oatmeal with Fresh Fruit
- Roasted Beet and Goat Cheese Salad
- Baked Cod with Tomato and Basil
- Sweet Potato and Black Bean Chili
- Quinoa Salad with Roasted Vegetables
- Poached Chicken with Herbs
- Spinach and Mushroom Omelette
- Mango and Avocado Salsa
- Broccoli and Cheese Stuffed Chicken
- Brown Rice and Lentil Pilaf
- Grilled Shrimp Skewers
- Greek Salad with Feta Cheese
- Baked Eggplant Parmesan
- Chicken and Vegetable Curry
- Kale and Berry Smoothie
- Roasted Brussels Sprouts with Balsamic Glaze
- Whole Wheat Banana Pancakes
- Zucchini Noodles with Pesto
- Black Bean and Corn Salad
- Salmon and Asparagus Foil Packets
- Quinoa and Black Bean Stuffed Peppers
- Turkey Meatballs with Marinara Sauce

- Lentil and Vegetable Soup
- Baked Halibut with Lemon and Garlic
- Chickpea and Spinach Curry
- Whole Wheat Berry Muffins
- Caprese Salad with Balsamic Reduction
- Turkey and Vegetable Skewers
- Roasted Cauliflower Steaks
- Mixed Berry Smoothie Bowl
- Mediterranean Grilled Chicken
- Ratatouille with Eggplant and Zucchini
- Baked Sweet Potato Fries
- Whole Grain Couscous Salad
- Chicken and Vegetable Kebabs
- Beet and Quinoa Salad

Grilled Salmon with Lemon and Dill

Ingredients:

- 4 salmon fillets, about 6 oz each, skin-on or skinless
- Salt and pepper, to taste
- 2 tablespoons olive oil
- 2 tablespoons fresh lemon juice
- Zest of 1 lemon
- 2 tablespoons fresh dill, chopped
- Lemon wedges, for serving

Instructions:

1. **Prepare the Salmon:**
    - Preheat your grill to medium-high heat. Alternatively, you can use a grill pan on the stove.
    - Pat the salmon fillets dry with paper towels. Season both sides with salt and pepper.
2. **Make the Marinade:**
    - In a small bowl, whisk together the olive oil, fresh lemon juice, lemon zest, and chopped dill.
3. **Grill the Salmon:**
    - Brush the grill grates lightly with oil to prevent sticking. Place the salmon fillets on the grill, flesh side down first if they have skin.
    - Grill for about 4-5 minutes on the first side, then carefully flip using a spatula. Grill for an additional 3-4 minutes on the second side, or until the salmon is cooked through and flakes easily with a fork. The internal temperature should reach 145°F (63°C).
4. **Serve:**
    - Transfer the grilled salmon to a serving platter or individual plates.
    - Drizzle the lemon dill marinade over the salmon fillets.
    - Garnish with additional fresh dill and serve with lemon wedges on the side.

Tips:

- **Grilling Tips:** To prevent the salmon from sticking to the grill, make sure it's properly preheated and lightly oiled. Start with the flesh side down if the salmon has skin.
- **Salmon Varieties:** You can use either skin-on or skinless salmon fillets for this recipe, depending on your preference.
- **Serving Suggestions:** Grilled salmon with lemon and dill pairs well with sides like steamed vegetables, roasted potatoes, or a fresh salad.

This Grilled Salmon with Lemon and Dill recipe is perfect for a healthy and flavorful meal that's quick to prepare and full of Omega-3 fatty acids, making it great for heart health.

Quinoa-Stuffed Bell Peppers

Ingredients:

- 4 large bell peppers (any color)
- 1 cup quinoa
- 2 cups vegetable broth or water
- 1 tablespoon olive oil
- 1 onion, diced
- 2 cloves garlic, minced
- 1 can (15 ounces) black beans, drained and rinsed
- 1 can (14.5 ounces) diced tomatoes, drained
- 1 cup corn kernels (fresh or frozen)
- 1 teaspoon cumin
- 1 teaspoon chili powder
- Salt and pepper to taste
- 1 cup shredded cheese (cheddar, mozzarella, or your choice)
- Fresh cilantro or parsley, chopped (optional, for garnish)

Instructions:

1. **Prepare the Quinoa:**
   - Rinse the quinoa under cold water to remove any bitterness.
   - In a saucepan, bring the vegetable broth or water to a boil.
   - Add the quinoa, reduce heat to low, cover, and simmer for about 15 minutes or until the quinoa is cooked and the liquid is absorbed. Remove from heat and fluff with a fork.
2. **Prepare the Bell Peppers:**
   - Preheat your oven to 375°F (190°C).
   - Cut the tops off the bell peppers and remove the seeds and membranes from inside.
   - Place the bell peppers upright in a baking dish that's been lightly greased with olive oil or cooking spray.
3. **Prepare the Filling:**
   - In a large skillet, heat olive oil over medium heat.
   - Add diced onion and cook until softened, about 5-7 minutes.
   - Add minced garlic and cook for another 1-2 minutes until fragrant.
4. **Assemble the Filling:**
   - To the skillet, add the cooked quinoa, black beans, diced tomatoes, corn kernels, cumin, chili powder, salt, and pepper. Stir well to combine and cook for another 5 minutes until heated through.
5. **Stuff the Bell Peppers:**
   - Spoon the quinoa mixture evenly into the prepared bell peppers, pressing down gently to pack the filling.

6. **Bake:**
    - Cover the baking dish with foil and bake in the preheated oven for 25-30 minutes, or until the bell peppers are tender.
7. **Add Cheese (Optional):**
    - Remove the foil, sprinkle shredded cheese over the tops of the stuffed peppers, and bake uncovered for another 5-10 minutes, or until the cheese is melted and bubbly.
8. **Serve:**
    - Remove from the oven and let cool slightly before serving.
    - Garnish with chopped cilantro or parsley if desired.

These quinoa-stuffed bell peppers are not only a great vegetarian dish but also a fantastic way to enjoy a balanced meal packed with protein, fiber, and flavor. Enjoy!

Mediterranean Chickpea Salad

Ingredients:

- 2 cans (15 ounces each) chickpeas, drained and rinsed
- 1 English cucumber, diced
- 1 pint cherry tomatoes, halved
- 1/2 red onion, thinly sliced
- 1/2 cup Kalamata olives, pitted and sliced
- 1/2 cup crumbled feta cheese
- 1/4 cup chopped fresh parsley
- 1/4 cup chopped fresh mint (optional)
- Juice of 1 lemon
- 3 tablespoons extra virgin olive oil
- 1 teaspoon dried oregano
- Salt and pepper, to taste

Instructions:

1. **Prepare the Chickpeas:**
   - Drain and rinse the chickpeas thoroughly under cold water. Transfer them to a large mixing bowl.
2. **Prepare the Vegetables:**
   - Dice the English cucumber into small pieces.
   - Halve the cherry tomatoes.
   - Thinly slice the red onion.
   - Slice the Kalamata olives.
3. **Combine Ingredients:**
   - Add the diced cucumber, halved cherry tomatoes, sliced red onion, sliced Kalamata olives, crumbled feta cheese, chopped parsley, and chopped mint (if using) to the bowl with the chickpeas.
4. **Make the Dressing:**
   - In a small bowl, whisk together the lemon juice, extra virgin olive oil, dried oregano, salt, and pepper until well combined.
5. **Assemble the Salad:**
   - Pour the dressing over the chickpea and vegetable mixture in the large bowl.
   - Gently toss everything together until all ingredients are evenly coated with the dressing.
6. **Chill and Serve:**
   - Refrigerate the salad for at least 30 minutes to allow the flavors to meld together.
   - Before serving, taste and adjust seasoning if needed.
   - Serve chilled, garnished with extra fresh herbs if desired.

Notes:

- This Mediterranean Chickpea Salad can be served on its own as a light meal, or as a side dish alongside grilled meats or seafood.
- It's a versatile recipe, so feel free to adjust the ingredients according to your taste preferences or what you have on hand.
- Leftovers can be stored in an airtight container in the refrigerator for up to 3 days.

Enjoy this Mediterranean-inspired salad packed with wholesome ingredients and vibrant flavors!

Baked Chicken with Herbs

Ingredients:

- 4 boneless, skinless chicken breasts
- 2 tablespoons olive oil
- 2 cloves garlic, minced
- 1 teaspoon dried thyme
- 1 teaspoon dried rosemary
- 1 teaspoon dried oregano
- 1/2 teaspoon dried sage
- Salt and pepper, to taste
- Juice of 1 lemon
- Fresh herbs for garnish (optional)

Instructions:

1. **Preheat the Oven:**
   - Preheat your oven to 400°F (200°C).
2. **Prepare the Chicken:**
   - Pat dry the chicken breasts with paper towels. This helps the chicken to brown better in the oven.
   - Season both sides of the chicken breasts with salt and pepper.
3. **Prepare the Herb Mixture:**
   - In a small bowl, combine the olive oil, minced garlic, dried thyme, dried rosemary, dried oregano, and dried sage. Mix well to create a herb-infused oil.
4. **Coat the Chicken:**
   - Brush or rub the herb mixture evenly over both sides of the chicken breasts. Make sure each breast is well coated with the herbs.
5. **Bake the Chicken:**
   - Place the seasoned chicken breasts in a baking dish or on a baking sheet lined with parchment paper.
   - Squeeze the juice of 1 lemon evenly over the chicken breasts.
6. **Bake in the Oven:**
   - Bake the chicken in the preheated oven for 20-25 minutes, or until the chicken is cooked through and reaches an internal temperature of 165°F (75°C).
7. **Rest and Serve:**
   - Once cooked, remove the chicken from the oven and let it rest for a few minutes.
   - Garnish with fresh herbs like parsley or thyme if desired before serving.
8. **Serve Warm:**
   - Serve the baked chicken breasts with your favorite side dishes like roasted vegetables, rice, or salad.

Tips:

- Make sure to adjust the baking time depending on the thickness of your chicken breasts. Thicker breasts may require a few extra minutes in the oven.
- You can add more garlic or adjust the amount of herbs to suit your taste preferences.
- Leftovers can be stored in an airtight container in the refrigerator for a few days and used in salads, wraps, or sandwiches.

This baked chicken with herbs recipe is perfect for a quick and flavorful dinner that's sure to satisfy!

Spinach and Kale Smoothie

Ingredients:

- 1 cup fresh spinach leaves
- 1 cup kale leaves, tough stems removed
- 1 banana, preferably frozen
- 1/2 cup frozen pineapple chunks
- 1/2 cup frozen mango chunks
- 1 tablespoon chia seeds or flax seeds (optional)
- 1 cup unsweetened almond milk or your choice of milk
- Honey or maple syrup, to taste (optional, for sweetness)
- Ice cubes (optional, for a colder smoothie)

Instructions:

1. **Prepare the Ingredients:**
    - Wash the spinach and kale leaves thoroughly. Remove any tough stems from the kale.
2. **Blend the Greens:**
    - In a blender, combine the spinach, kale, banana, frozen pineapple chunks, frozen mango chunks, and chia or flax seeds (if using).
3. **Add Liquid:**
    - Pour in the almond milk or your preferred type of milk.
4. **Sweeten (Optional):**
    - If you prefer a sweeter smoothie, add honey or maple syrup to taste.
5. **Blend Until Smooth:**
    - Blend all the ingredients until smooth and creamy. If you prefer a thicker smoothie, you can add more frozen fruits or ice cubes.
6. **Adjust Consistency:**
    - If the smoothie is too thick, add a little more almond milk. If it's too thin, add more frozen fruits or ice cubes.
7. **Serve:**
    - Pour the spinach and kale smoothie into glasses and serve immediately.

Tips:

- You can customize this smoothie based on your preferences. Feel free to swap the fruits with others like berries, apples, or pears.
- For added protein, you can blend in a scoop of protein powder or Greek yogurt.
- To make it more nutrient-dense, consider adding a handful of nuts or seeds such as almonds, walnuts, or hemp seeds.
- Leftover smoothie can be stored in the refrigerator for up to 1 day in an airtight container. Shake or stir well before drinking.

This spinach and kale smoothie is packed with vitamins, minerals, and fiber, making it a great choice for a healthy breakfast or snack that will keep you energized throughout the day!

Lentil Soup with Vegetables

Ingredients:

- 1 cup dried lentils (brown or green), rinsed and picked over
- 1 tablespoon olive oil
- 1 onion, diced
- 2 carrots, diced
- 2 celery stalks, diced
- 3 cloves garlic, minced
- 1 teaspoon ground cumin
- 1 teaspoon ground coriander
- 1/2 teaspoon smoked paprika (optional, for extra flavor)
- 6 cups vegetable broth or water
- 1 can (14.5 ounces) diced tomatoes
- 2 cups chopped spinach or kale
- Salt and pepper, to taste
- Juice of 1 lemon (optional, for brightness)
- Fresh parsley or cilantro, chopped (for garnish)

Instructions:

1. **Prepare the Lentils:**
   - Rinse the lentils under cold water and pick over to remove any debris. Set aside.
2. **Saute Vegetables:**
   - In a large pot or Dutch oven, heat the olive oil over medium heat.
   - Add the diced onion, carrots, and celery. Cook, stirring occasionally, until the vegetables start to soften, about 5-7 minutes.
3. **Add Garlic and Spices:**
   - Stir in the minced garlic, ground cumin, ground coriander, and smoked paprika (if using). Cook for 1-2 minutes until fragrant.
4. **Cook Lentils:**
   - Add the rinsed lentils to the pot and stir to combine with the vegetables and spices.
5. **Add Broth and Tomatoes:**
   - Pour in the vegetable broth (or water) and diced tomatoes with their juices. Bring the mixture to a boil.
6. **Simmer:**
   - Reduce the heat to low, cover the pot partially with a lid, and simmer for about 20-25 minutes, or until the lentils are tender.
7. **Add Greens:**
   - Stir in the chopped spinach or kale and cook for an additional 5 minutes until the greens are wilted and tender.
8. **Season and Finish:**

- Season the soup with salt and pepper to taste. If desired, add a squeeze of lemon juice for brightness.
9. **Serve:**
    - Ladle the lentil soup into bowls and garnish with chopped fresh parsley or cilantro.

Tips:

- You can customize this lentil soup by adding other vegetables such as bell peppers, zucchini, or potatoes.
- For a creamier texture, you can blend a portion of the soup with an immersion blender before adding the greens.
- Leftover soup can be stored in an airtight container in the refrigerator for up to 4-5 days or frozen for longer storage. Reheat gently on the stove or in the microwave.

Enjoy this wholesome lentil soup with vegetables as a satisfying meal that's packed with protein, fiber, and essential nutrients!

Whole Wheat Pasta Primavera

Ingredients:

- 12 ounces whole wheat pasta (such as penne or spaghetti)
- 2 tablespoons olive oil
- 3 cloves garlic, minced
- 1 onion, thinly sliced
- 1 red bell pepper, thinly sliced
- 1 yellow bell pepper, thinly sliced
- 1 zucchini, halved lengthwise and sliced
- 1 yellow squash, halved lengthwise and sliced
- 1 cup cherry tomatoes, halved
- 1 cup broccoli florets
- 1/2 cup vegetable broth or pasta cooking water
- 1/2 cup grated Parmesan cheese (optional)
- Salt and pepper, to taste
- Fresh basil or parsley, chopped, for garnish

Instructions:

1. **Cook the Pasta:**
    - Cook the whole wheat pasta according to the package instructions in a large pot of salted boiling water until al dente. Reserve 1/2 cup of pasta cooking water before draining.
2. **Prepare the Vegetables:**
    - While the pasta is cooking, heat olive oil in a large skillet over medium heat.
    - Add minced garlic and sauté for about 1 minute until fragrant.
3. **Saute Vegetables:**
    - Add the sliced onion, red bell pepper, yellow bell pepper, zucchini, yellow squash, cherry tomatoes, and broccoli florets to the skillet.
    - Cook, stirring occasionally, for about 5-7 minutes or until the vegetables are tender-crisp.
4. **Combine Pasta and Vegetables:**
    - Add the cooked whole wheat pasta to the skillet with the sautéed vegetables.
    - Pour in the vegetable broth or reserved pasta cooking water to help create a sauce. Stir well to combine.
5. **Season and Finish:**
    - Season the pasta primavera with salt and pepper to taste.
    - If using, sprinkle grated Parmesan cheese over the pasta and toss until well combined and heated through.
6. **Garnish and Serve:**
    - Remove from heat and garnish with chopped fresh basil or parsley.
7. **Serve Warm:**

- Divide the whole wheat pasta primavera into plates or bowls.
- Serve immediately, optionally garnished with additional Parmesan cheese and fresh herbs.

Tips:

- Feel free to customize the vegetables based on what's in season or what you have on hand.
- You can add a splash of white wine or lemon juice to the skillet while cooking the vegetables for extra flavor.
- For a creamier sauce, you can stir in a little cream or a dollop of Greek yogurt at the end.

This whole wheat pasta primavera is a wholesome and satisfying meal that's loaded with fiber, vitamins, and minerals from the colorful array of vegetables. Enjoy!

Grilled Vegetable Skewers

Ingredients:

- Assorted vegetables, such as:
    - Cherry tomatoes
    - Bell peppers (red, yellow, and/or green), cut into chunks
    - Zucchini, sliced into rounds or half moons
    - Yellow squash, sliced into rounds or half moons
    - Red onion, cut into wedges
    - Mushrooms (button or cremini), whole or halved depending on size
- Wooden or metal skewers (if using wooden skewers, soak them in water for at least 30 minutes to prevent burning)
- Olive oil
- Salt and pepper, to taste
- Fresh herbs (optional), such as rosemary or thyme, for garnish

Instructions:

1. **Prepare the Vegetables:**
    - Wash and prepare all the vegetables. Cut them into pieces that are roughly the same size so they cook evenly on the grill.
2. **Assemble the Skewers:**
    - Thread the vegetables onto skewers, alternating different types and colors for a visually appealing presentation.
3. **Brush with Olive Oil:**
    - Place the assembled skewers on a baking sheet or tray. Brush them generously with olive oil on all sides.
4. **Season:**
    - Season the skewers with salt and pepper, to taste. You can also sprinkle them with dried herbs or seasoning blends if desired.
5. **Preheat the Grill:**
    - Preheat your grill to medium-high heat. Make sure the grates are clean and lightly oiled to prevent sticking.
6. **Grill the Skewers:**
    - Place the vegetable skewers on the grill and cook for about 8-10 minutes, turning occasionally, until the vegetables are tender and have grill marks.
7. **Serve:**
    - Remove the skewers from the grill and transfer them to a serving platter.
    - Garnish with fresh herbs like chopped rosemary or thyme, if desired, and serve immediately.

Tips:

- **Marinate:** You can marinate the vegetables in a mixture of olive oil, balsamic vinegar, garlic, and herbs before threading them onto skewers for extra flavor.
- **Variations:** Feel free to add other vegetables like eggplant, asparagus, or cherry peppers to the skewers based on your preferences.
- **Grill Preparation:** Ensure your grill is hot enough to create those nice grill marks without burning the vegetables. Adjust the heat as needed during grilling.

These grilled vegetable skewers are not only delicious but also a healthy addition to any meal. They can be served as a side dish, a vegetarian main course, or alongside grilled meats for a complete barbecue feast. Enjoy!

Avocado and Black Bean Salad

Ingredients:

- 1 can (15 ounces) black beans, drained and rinsed
- 2 ripe avocados, diced
- 1 cup cherry tomatoes, halved
- 1/2 red onion, finely diced
- 1/4 cup fresh cilantro, chopped
- Juice of 1 lime
- 2 tablespoons olive oil
- 1 teaspoon ground cumin
- Salt and pepper, to taste
- Optional: 1 jalapeño pepper, seeded and finely diced (for a spicy kick)

Instructions:

1. **Prepare the Dressing:**
   - In a small bowl, whisk together the lime juice, olive oil, ground cumin, salt, and pepper. Set aside.
2. **Combine Ingredients:**
   - In a large mixing bowl, combine the black beans, diced avocado, cherry tomatoes, finely diced red onion, chopped cilantro, and jalapeño pepper (if using).
3. **Add Dressing:**
   - Pour the dressing over the salad ingredients in the bowl.
4. **Mix Gently:**
   - Gently toss everything together until well combined, being careful not to mash the avocado.
5. **Adjust Seasoning:**
   - Taste and adjust seasoning with additional salt, pepper, or lime juice as needed.
6. **Chill (Optional):**
   - You can chill the salad in the refrigerator for about 30 minutes to let the flavors meld together before serving.
7. **Serve:**
   - Serve the avocado and black bean salad chilled or at room temperature.

Tips:

- **Variations:** Feel free to add other ingredients such as corn kernels, diced bell peppers, or quinoa to make the salad more substantial.
- **Storage:** Avocado can brown over time, so if you're making the salad ahead of time, add the avocado just before serving and store any leftovers in an airtight container in the refrigerator for up to 1 day.

- **Serving Suggestions:** This salad pairs well with grilled chicken or fish, and it's also delicious as a filling for tacos or wraps.

This avocado and black bean salad is packed with fiber, healthy fats, and fresh flavors, making it a satisfying and nutritious addition to any meal!

Turkey and Vegetable Stir-Fry

Ingredients:

- 1 lb turkey breast or turkey tenderloin, thinly sliced
- 2 tablespoons soy sauce
- 1 tablespoon oyster sauce (optional, for added umami)
- 1 tablespoon cornstarch
- 1 tablespoon vegetable oil
- 2 cloves garlic, minced
- 1 inch piece of ginger, grated or minced
- 1 onion, thinly sliced
- 1 bell pepper (any color), thinly sliced
- 1 zucchini, halved lengthwise and sliced
- 1 cup broccoli florets
- 1 carrot, thinly sliced
- 1 cup snap peas or snow peas
- Salt and pepper, to taste
- Cooked rice or noodles, for serving
- Sesame seeds and chopped green onions, for garnish (optional)

Instructions:

1. **Prepare the Turkey:**
   - In a bowl, combine the sliced turkey with soy sauce, oyster sauce (if using), and cornstarch. Mix well to coat the turkey evenly. Let it marinate for about 10-15 minutes.
2. **Heat the Oil:**
   - Heat vegetable oil in a large skillet or wok over medium-high heat.
3. **Stir-Fry the Turkey:**
   - Add the marinated turkey to the hot skillet. Stir-fry for 3-4 minutes, or until the turkey is cooked through and lightly browned. Remove the turkey from the skillet and set aside.
4. **Cook the Vegetables:**
   - In the same skillet, add a bit more oil if needed. Add minced garlic and grated ginger. Cook for about 1 minute until fragrant.
   - Add the sliced onion, bell pepper, zucchini, broccoli florets, carrot, and snap peas/snow peas to the skillet. Stir-fry for 4-5 minutes, or until the vegetables are tender-crisp.
5. **Combine and Season:**
   - Return the cooked turkey to the skillet with the vegetables. Stir everything together to combine.
   - Season with salt and pepper to taste. Adjust the seasoning if needed.
6. **Serve:**

- Serve the turkey and vegetable stir-fry hot over cooked rice or noodles.
- Garnish with sesame seeds and chopped green onions, if desired.

Tips:

- **Variations:** Feel free to add other vegetables such as mushrooms, baby corn, or bok choy.
- **Sauce:** If you prefer a saucier stir-fry, you can add a mixture of soy sauce, oyster sauce, and a little chicken broth or water to the skillet after cooking the vegetables.
- **Spice it Up:** Add a pinch of red pepper flakes or a dash of Sriracha for a bit of heat.

This turkey and vegetable stir-fry is a wholesome and satisfying meal that's perfect for a quick weeknight dinner. Enjoy the tender turkey and crisp vegetables in a flavorful sauce over your choice of rice or noodles!

Roasted Garlic and White Bean Dip

Ingredients:

- 1 head of garlic
- 1 tablespoon olive oil
- 1 can (15 ounces) white beans (such as cannellini or great northern beans), drained and rinsed
- 2 tablespoons tahini (sesame seed paste)
- Juice of 1 lemon
- 2 tablespoons olive oil
- 1/2 teaspoon ground cumin
- Salt and pepper, to taste
- Water (as needed for desired consistency)
- Optional garnishes: chopped fresh parsley, paprika, extra olive oil

Instructions:

1. **Roast the Garlic:**
   - Preheat the oven to 400°F (200°C).
   - Peel away the outer layers of the garlic bulb skin, leaving the cloves intact and keeping the bulb whole. Cut off the top of the bulb, exposing the cloves inside.
   - Drizzle the exposed cloves with olive oil, then wrap the bulb loosely in aluminum foil. Place it on a baking sheet and roast in the preheated oven for about 30-35 minutes, or until the cloves are soft and golden brown. Remove from the oven and let cool.
2. **Prepare the Dip:**
   - Once the roasted garlic is cool enough to handle, squeeze the cloves out of their skins into a food processor or blender.
3. **Blend Ingredients:**
   - Add the drained and rinsed white beans, tahini, lemon juice, olive oil, ground cumin, salt, and pepper to the food processor or blender with the roasted garlic.
4. **Blend until Smooth:**
   - Process or blend until the mixture is smooth and creamy. If the dip is too thick, add water, a tablespoon at a time, until you reach your desired consistency.
5. **Adjust Seasoning:**
   - Taste and adjust the seasoning with more salt, pepper, or lemon juice as needed.
6. **Serve:**
   - Transfer the roasted garlic and white bean dip to a serving bowl. Drizzle with a little extra olive oil and sprinkle with chopped fresh parsley or a pinch of paprika for garnish, if desired.
7. **Enjoy:**
   - Serve the dip with fresh vegetables, pita bread, crackers, or chips.

Tips:

- **Variations:** You can customize this dip by adding herbs like fresh parsley or basil, or spices like paprika or chili flakes for extra flavor.
- **Storage:** Store any leftover dip in an airtight container in the refrigerator for up to 4-5 days. Stir well before serving again.

This roasted garlic and white bean dip is creamy, savory, and packed with the delicious flavor of roasted garlic. It's a great appetizer or snack that's sure to be a hit at any gathering!

Cauliflower Rice Stir-Fry

Ingredients:

- 1 medium head of cauliflower
- 2 tablespoons vegetable oil or sesame oil
- 2 cloves garlic, minced
- 1 tablespoon fresh ginger, grated or minced
- 1 onion, diced
- 1 bell pepper (any color), diced
- 1 carrot, diced
- 1 cup broccoli florets
- 1 cup snap peas or snow peas
- 2-3 tablespoons soy sauce (adjust to taste)
- 1 tablespoon oyster sauce (optional, for extra flavor)
- Salt and pepper, to taste
- Optional protein: cooked chicken, shrimp, tofu, or edamame
- Green onions, chopped, for garnish
- Sesame seeds, for garnish

Instructions:

1. **Prepare the Cauliflower Rice:**
    - Remove the leaves and core from the cauliflower head. Cut the cauliflower into florets.
    - Working in batches, pulse the cauliflower florets in a food processor until they resemble rice-like grains. Be careful not to over-process into mush. Alternatively, you can use a box grater to grate the cauliflower into rice-like pieces.
2. **Stir-Fry the Vegetables:**
    - Heat 1 tablespoon of oil in a large skillet or wok over medium-high heat.
    - Add minced garlic and grated ginger. Cook for about 1 minute until fragrant.
    - Add diced onion, bell pepper, carrot, broccoli florets, and snap peas/snow peas to the skillet. Stir-fry for 4-5 minutes, or until the vegetables are tender-crisp. Remove the vegetables from the skillet and set aside.
3. **Cook the Cauliflower Rice:**
    - In the same skillet, heat the remaining 1 tablespoon of oil over medium heat.
    - Add the cauliflower rice to the skillet. Stir-fry for 5-6 minutes, stirring frequently, until the cauliflower is tender and slightly golden.
4. **Combine and Season:**
    - Return the cooked vegetables to the skillet with the cauliflower rice.
    - Add soy sauce and oyster sauce (if using). Stir well to combine and heat through.
    - Season with salt and pepper to taste. Adjust seasoning if needed.
5. **Add Protein (Optional):**

- If adding protein such as cooked chicken, shrimp, tofu, or edamame, add it to the skillet with the cauliflower rice and vegetables. Stir to combine and heat through.
6. **Serve:**
    - Serve the cauliflower rice stir-fry hot, garnished with chopped green onions and sesame seeds.

Tips:

- **Variations:** Feel free to add other vegetables such as mushrooms, cabbage, or baby corn.
- **Sauce:** You can customize the sauce with additional ingredients like hoisin sauce, rice vinegar, or chili sauce for extra flavor.
- **Make it Spicy:** Add a pinch of red pepper flakes or a dash of Sriracha for heat.

This cauliflower rice stir-fry is a delicious and nutritious alternative to traditional stir-fries, offering a lighter option that's packed with vegetables and flavor. Enjoy it as a main dish or as a tasty side!

Greek Yogurt Parfait with Berries

Ingredients:

- 1 cup Greek yogurt (plain or vanilla flavored)
- 1 cup mixed berries (such as strawberries, blueberries, raspberries)
- 1/2 cup granola (homemade or store-bought)
- 1-2 tablespoons honey or maple syrup (optional, for added sweetness)
- Fresh mint leaves, for garnish (optional)

Instructions:

1. **Prepare the Berries:**
   - Rinse the berries under cold water and pat them dry with a paper towel. If using strawberries, hull them and slice them into smaller pieces if desired.
2. **Assemble the Parfait:**
   - Start by layering a spoonful of Greek yogurt into the bottom of a glass or parfait dish.
   - Add a layer of mixed berries on top of the yogurt.
3. **Add Granola:**
   - Sprinkle a layer of granola over the berries.
4. **Repeat Layers:**
   - Repeat the layers: yogurt, berries, and granola until you reach the top of the glass or dish.
5. **Drizzle with Honey (Optional):**
   - If you prefer a sweeter parfait, drizzle honey or maple syrup over the top layer of yogurt and berries.
6. **Garnish and Serve:**
   - Garnish with fresh mint leaves for a pop of color and extra freshness.
7. **Enjoy Immediately:**
   - Serve the Greek yogurt parfait immediately to enjoy the crunchy granola, creamy yogurt, and juicy berries at their best.

Tips:

- **Variations:** Feel free to customize your parfait with different fruits such as bananas, peaches, or kiwi. You can also use flavored Greek yogurt or mix in some chia seeds or nuts for added texture.
- **Make it Vegan:** Use dairy-free yogurt alternatives like almond or coconut yogurt and substitute honey with agave syrup or another vegan sweetener.
- **Preparation Ahead:** You can prepare the components of the parfait (yogurt, berries, and granola) ahead of time and assemble just before serving to keep the granola crunchy.

This Greek yogurt parfait with berries is not only delicious but also nutritious, providing a good balance of protein, fiber, vitamins, and antioxidants. It's a versatile dish that's sure to satisfy your cravings for something sweet and refreshing!

Tuna and White Bean Salad

Ingredients:

- 1 can (15 ounces) white beans (such as cannellini beans or navy beans), drained and rinsed
- 1 can (5 ounces) tuna in water or olive oil, drained
- 1/2 red onion, finely chopped
- 1 celery stalk, finely chopped
- 1/2 cup cherry tomatoes, halved
- 1/4 cup chopped fresh parsley
- 2 tablespoons extra virgin olive oil
- Juice of 1 lemon
- Salt and pepper, to taste
- Optional: 1 tablespoon capers or chopped olives for added flavor
- Optional: Mixed salad greens or lettuce leaves for serving

Instructions:

1. **Prepare the Salad Base:**
   - In a large mixing bowl, combine the drained and rinsed white beans, drained tuna, chopped red onion, celery, cherry tomatoes, and chopped parsley.
2. **Make the Dressing:**
   - In a small bowl, whisk together the extra virgin olive oil, lemon juice, salt, and pepper. Adjust the seasoning to taste.
3. **Combine and Toss:**
   - Pour the dressing over the tuna and white bean mixture in the bowl. Add capers or chopped olives if using. Gently toss everything together until well combined and evenly coated with the dressing.
4. **Serve:**
   - Serve the tuna and white bean salad immediately as is, or spoon it over a bed of mixed salad greens or lettuce leaves for a lighter presentation.

Tips:

- **Variations:** Feel free to add other ingredients like diced cucumber, bell peppers, or avocado for extra flavor and texture.
- **Make it Creamy:** If you prefer a creamier salad, you can mix in a tablespoon or two of Greek yogurt or mayonnaise to the dressing.
- **Storage:** Store any leftover salad in an airtight container in the refrigerator for up to 2-3 days. The flavors will meld together nicely over time.

This tuna and white bean salad is not only quick and easy to prepare but also nutritious and satisfying. It's perfect for a healthy lunch or a light dinner option!

Oatmeal with Fresh Fruit

Ingredients:

- 1/2 cup old-fashioned rolled oats
- 1 cup water or milk (dairy or plant-based)
- Pinch of salt
- 1/2 teaspoon vanilla extract (optional)
- Fresh fruit of your choice, such as:
    - Sliced strawberries
    - Blueberries
    - Sliced bananas
    - Raspberries
    - Sliced peaches or nectarines
- Optional toppings:
    - Honey or maple syrup, for sweetness
    - Chopped nuts (such as almonds, walnuts, or pecans)
    - Seeds (such as chia seeds, flax seeds, or pumpkin seeds)
    - Yogurt or nut butter for added creaminess

Instructions:

1. **Cook the Oatmeal:**
    - In a small saucepan, bring the water or milk to a boil over medium-high heat.
2. **Add Oats and Cook:**
    - Stir in the rolled oats and a pinch of salt. Reduce the heat to medium-low and simmer, stirring occasionally, for about 5-7 minutes or until the oats are tender and have absorbed most of the liquid. Stir in vanilla extract if using.
3. **Prepare the Fruit:**
    - While the oatmeal is cooking, prepare your fresh fruit by washing and slicing as needed.
4. **Assemble the Oatmeal Bowl:**
    - Once the oatmeal is cooked to your desired consistency, remove the saucepan from the heat.
5. **Add Fresh Fruit:**
    - Spoon the cooked oatmeal into a serving bowl. Top with your choice of fresh fruit.
6. **Optional Toppings:**
    - Drizzle honey or maple syrup over the oatmeal and fruit for added sweetness, if desired.
    - Sprinkle chopped nuts and seeds over the top for added crunch and nutrition.
    - Add a dollop of yogurt or a swirl of nut butter for extra creaminess and protein.
7. **Serve Immediately:**
    - Serve the oatmeal with fresh fruit immediately while it's warm.

Tips:

- **Variations:** Feel free to customize your oatmeal with different combinations of fruits and toppings based on your preferences and what's in season.
- **Make it Overnight Oats:** If you prefer a cold version, you can make overnight oats by soaking rolled oats in milk or yogurt overnight in the refrigerator. In the morning, top with fresh fruit and enjoy.
- **Nutritional Boost:** For extra nutrition, consider adding superfoods like goji berries, hemp seeds, or acai berries.

This oatmeal with fresh fruit is a nutritious and satisfying way to start your day, providing you with energy and essential nutrients. It's versatile and can be tailored to suit your taste preferences, making it a breakfast option that's both delicious and wholesome!

Roasted Beet and Goat Cheese Salad

Ingredients:

- 3 medium beets, preferably mixed colors (red, golden, or chioggia)
- 4 ounces goat cheese, crumbled
- 4 cups mixed salad greens (such as baby spinach, arugula, or mixed greens)
- 1/4 cup walnuts, toasted and chopped
- 2 tablespoons balsamic vinegar
- 2 tablespoons extra virgin olive oil
- 1 teaspoon Dijon mustard
- Salt and pepper, to taste

Instructions:

1. **Roast the Beets:**
    - Preheat your oven to 400°F (200°C).
    - Wash and trim the beets, leaving the root and about 1 inch of the stems attached. This helps retain their color and prevents bleeding.
    - Wrap each beet individually in aluminum foil and place them on a baking sheet.
    - Roast in the preheated oven for 45-60 minutes, or until the beets are tender when pierced with a fork.
    - Once roasted, let the beets cool slightly, then peel off the skins using a paper towel (they should slide off easily). Cut the beets into wedges or slices.
2. **Prepare the Salad Dressing:**
    - In a small bowl, whisk together balsamic vinegar, olive oil, Dijon mustard, salt, and pepper until well combined. Adjust seasoning to taste.
3. **Assemble the Salad:**
    - In a large mixing bowl, toss the mixed salad greens with half of the dressing until evenly coated.
    - Arrange the dressed greens on a serving platter or individual plates.
    - Top with roasted beet slices or wedges.
    - Scatter crumbled goat cheese and toasted chopped walnuts over the salad.
4. **Finish and Serve:**
    - Drizzle the remaining dressing over the salad.
    - Optionally, garnish with additional walnuts and a few sprigs of fresh herbs like parsley or thyme.
    - Serve the roasted beet and goat cheese salad immediately as a delicious and nutritious appetizer or main course.

Tips:

- **Variations:** You can add additional ingredients such as sliced oranges, pomegranate seeds, or avocado for extra flavor and texture.

- **Make Ahead:** You can roast the beets ahead of time and store them in the refrigerator. Assemble the salad just before serving to keep the greens fresh.
- **Vegan Option:** To make this salad vegan, substitute the goat cheese with a dairy-free cheese alternative or omit it altogether.

This roasted beet and goat cheese salad is not only visually stunning but also full of flavors and textures that complement each other perfectly. It's a great dish for any occasion, whether you're hosting a dinner party or enjoying a light lunch!

Baked Cod with Tomato and Basil

Ingredients:

- 4 cod fillets (about 6 ounces each), skinless
- Salt and pepper, to taste
- 2 tablespoons olive oil
- 2 cloves garlic, minced
- 1 pint cherry tomatoes, halved
- 1/4 cup fresh basil leaves, chopped
- 1 tablespoon balsamic vinegar
- 1/4 teaspoon red pepper flakes (optional, for a bit of heat)
- Lemon wedges, for serving
- Fresh basil leaves, for garnish (optional)

Instructions:

1. **Preheat the Oven:**
   - Preheat your oven to 400°F (200°C).
2. **Prepare the Cod Fillets:**
   - Pat the cod fillets dry with paper towels. Season both sides with salt and pepper.
3. **Sear the Cod:**
   - In a large oven-safe skillet or baking dish, heat olive oil over medium-high heat. Add the cod fillets and sear for 2-3 minutes on each side until lightly browned. Remove the cod from the skillet and set aside.
4. **Make the Tomato Basil Topping:**
   - In the same skillet, add minced garlic and sauté for about 1 minute until fragrant.
   - Add halved cherry tomatoes, chopped basil, balsamic vinegar, and red pepper flakes (if using). Season with salt and pepper to taste. Stir to combine.
5. **Bake the Cod:**
   - Return the seared cod fillets to the skillet, nestling them into the tomato basil mixture.
6. **Bake in the Oven:**
   - Transfer the skillet to the preheated oven and bake for 10-12 minutes, or until the cod is opaque and flakes easily with a fork.
7. **Serve:**
   - Remove the baked cod from the oven. Serve hot, garnished with fresh basil leaves and lemon wedges on the side.

Tips:

- **Side Dish Suggestions:** This dish pairs well with steamed vegetables, roasted potatoes, or a side salad.

- **Variations:** You can customize the recipe by adding olives, capers, or diced bell peppers to the tomato basil topping for additional flavors.
- **Freshness:** For the best flavor, use fresh basil and ripe cherry tomatoes.

This baked cod with tomato and basil is a simple yet elegant dish that's perfect for a quick weeknight dinner or a special occasion. Enjoy the tender cod with the burst of flavors from the tomato and basil topping!

Sweet Potato and Black Bean Chili

Ingredients:

- 2 tablespoons olive oil
- 1 large onion, diced
- 3 cloves garlic, minced
- 1 large sweet potato, peeled and diced into 1/2-inch cubes
- 1 red bell pepper, diced
- 1 jalapeño pepper, seeded and minced (optional, for heat)
- 1 tablespoon chili powder
- 1 teaspoon ground cumin
- 1/2 teaspoon smoked paprika
- 1/2 teaspoon dried oregano
- 1/4 teaspoon cayenne pepper (optional, for additional heat)
- Salt and pepper, to taste
- 1 (15 oz) can black beans, drained and rinsed
- 1 (15 oz) can diced tomatoes
- 2 cups vegetable broth or chicken broth
- 1 cup frozen corn kernels
- Juice of 1 lime
- Fresh cilantro, chopped, for garnish
- Avocado slices, for serving (optional)
- Sour cream or Greek yogurt, for serving (optional)

Instructions:

1. **Sauté aromatics and vegetables:**
   - In a large pot or Dutch oven, heat olive oil over medium heat. Add diced onion and cook until softened, about 5 minutes.
   - Add minced garlic, diced sweet potato, diced red bell pepper, and minced jalapeño pepper (if using). Sauté for another 5 minutes, stirring occasionally.
2. **Add spices:**
   - Stir in chili powder, ground cumin, smoked paprika, dried oregano, cayenne pepper (if using), salt, and pepper. Cook for 1-2 minutes until fragrant, stirring constantly.
3. **Simmer chili:**
   - Add black beans, diced tomatoes (with their juices), and vegetable or chicken broth to the pot. Bring to a boil, then reduce heat to low. Cover and simmer for 15-20 minutes, or until sweet potatoes are tender.
4. **Add corn and lime juice:**
   - Stir in frozen corn kernels and cook for an additional 5 minutes, or until corn is heated through.

- Remove the pot from heat and stir in fresh lime juice. Taste and adjust seasoning if needed.
5. **Serve:**
    - Ladle the sweet potato and black bean chili into bowls. Garnish with chopped fresh cilantro.
    - Serve with avocado slices, sour cream or Greek yogurt on the side if desired.

Tips:

- **Make it vegan:** Use vegetable broth and skip the optional sour cream or Greek yogurt for a vegan-friendly dish.
- **Customize:** Add additional vegetables such as zucchini or spinach for extra nutrition and flavor.
- **Storage:** Leftover chili can be stored in an airtight container in the refrigerator for up to 4 days or frozen for up to 3 months. Reheat gently on the stovetop or in the microwave.

This sweet potato and black bean chili is nutritious, flavorful, and perfect for a cozy dinner. Enjoy it with your favorite toppings and crusty bread or cornbread on the side!

Quinoa Salad with Roasted Vegetables

Ingredients:

- 1 cup quinoa, rinsed
- 2 cups water or vegetable broth
- 1 small sweet potato, peeled and diced
- 1 red bell pepper, diced
- 1 zucchini, diced
- 1 small red onion, thinly sliced
- 2 tablespoons olive oil
- 1 teaspoon smoked paprika
- 1/2 teaspoon ground cumin
- Salt and pepper, to taste
- 1/4 cup fresh parsley or cilantro, chopped
- 1/4 cup crumbled feta cheese or goat cheese (optional)

For the dressing:

- 3 tablespoons olive oil
- 2 tablespoons balsamic vinegar
- 1 tablespoon Dijon mustard
- 1 clove garlic, minced
- Salt and pepper, to taste

Instructions:

1. **Roast the vegetables:**
    - Preheat your oven to 400°F (200°C).
    - In a large bowl, toss the diced sweet potato, red bell pepper, zucchini, and red onion with olive oil, smoked paprika, ground cumin, salt, and pepper until evenly coated.
    - Spread the vegetables in a single layer on a baking sheet lined with parchment paper. Roast in the preheated oven for 20-25 minutes, or until vegetables are tender and slightly caramelized. Stir halfway through cooking for even roasting.
2. **Cook the quinoa:**
    - While the vegetables are roasting, rinse the quinoa under cold water using a fine mesh sieve to remove any bitterness.
    - In a medium saucepan, bring 2 cups of water or vegetable broth to a boil. Add the rinsed quinoa and reduce the heat to low. Cover and simmer for 15 minutes, or until the quinoa is cooked and the liquid is absorbed. Remove from heat and let it sit, covered, for 5 minutes. Fluff with a fork.
3. **Prepare the dressing:**

- In a small bowl, whisk together olive oil, balsamic vinegar, Dijon mustard, minced garlic, salt, and pepper until well combined.
4. **Assemble the salad:**
    - In a large mixing bowl, combine the cooked quinoa and roasted vegetables.
    - Pour the dressing over the quinoa and vegetables. Toss gently to combine, ensuring everything is evenly coated with the dressing.
5. **Add finishing touches:**
    - Sprinkle chopped fresh parsley or cilantro over the salad. If using, sprinkle crumbled feta cheese or goat cheese on top for extra flavor.
6. **Serve:**
    - Serve the quinoa salad with roasted vegetables warm or at room temperature as a satisfying main dish or a hearty side.

Tips:

- **Variations:** Feel free to add other roasted vegetables such as cherry tomatoes, eggplant, or mushrooms to suit your taste.
- **Make ahead:** You can prepare the quinoa and roast the vegetables ahead of time. Store them separately in the refrigerator and assemble the salad just before serving.
- **Storage:** Leftover quinoa salad can be stored in an airtight container in the refrigerator for up to 3-4 days. The flavors will meld together nicely over time.

This quinoa salad with roasted vegetables is not only delicious but also packed with nutrients and perfect for a wholesome lunch or dinner. Enjoy the blend of flavors and textures in every bite!

Poached Chicken with Herbs

Ingredients:

- 4 boneless, skinless chicken breasts (about 1.5 pounds)
- 4 cups chicken broth (homemade or low-sodium store-bought)
- 2-3 sprigs of fresh herbs (such as thyme, rosemary, or parsley)
- 2 cloves garlic, smashed
- 1 lemon, sliced
- Salt and pepper, to taste

Optional garnishes:

- Fresh herbs (parsley, cilantro, or basil), chopped
- Lemon wedges

Instructions:

1. **Prepare the poaching liquid:**
   - In a large pot or deep skillet, combine the chicken broth, fresh herbs, smashed garlic cloves, and lemon slices. Bring to a gentle simmer over medium heat.
2. **Poach the chicken:**
   - Season the chicken breasts with salt and pepper on both sides.
   - Carefully add the chicken breasts to the simmering broth, ensuring they are fully submerged. If necessary, you can add a bit more broth or water to cover the chicken.
   - Reduce the heat to low to maintain a gentle simmer. Cover the pot partially with a lid.
3. **Cook the chicken:**
   - Poach the chicken for about 15-20 minutes, or until the internal temperature reaches 165°F (75°C) and the chicken is cooked through. Cooking time may vary depending on the thickness of the chicken breasts.
4. **Remove and rest:**
   - Once cooked, use tongs to carefully remove the chicken breasts from the poaching liquid and transfer them to a cutting board. Let the chicken rest for a few minutes before slicing or serving.
5. **Serve:**
   - Slice the poached chicken breasts crosswise into strips or dice them into cubes, as desired.
   - Arrange the chicken on a serving platter or individual plates.
   - Garnish with chopped fresh herbs and lemon wedges, if desired.
   - Serve the poached chicken with herbs hot or at room temperature.

Tips:

- **Flavor variations:** Feel free to customize the poaching liquid with additional herbs like sage or tarragon, or spices such as peppercorns or bay leaves.
- **Serve with sides:** Poached chicken with herbs pairs well with steamed vegetables, rice, quinoa, or a fresh salad.
- **Make ahead:** You can poach the chicken ahead of time and store it in the refrigerator in an airtight container for up to 3 days. Reheat gently in a skillet with a bit of broth or water to maintain moisture.

This poached chicken with herbs recipe is versatile and perfect for a light meal or as a base for other dishes like salads or sandwiches. Enjoy the tender and flavorful chicken with the aromatic essence of fresh herbs!

Spinach and Mushroom Omelette

Ingredients:

- 3 large eggs
- 1/4 cup milk or water
- Salt and pepper, to taste
- 1 tablespoon butter or olive oil
- 1 cup sliced mushrooms (button or cremini)
- 1 cup fresh spinach leaves, roughly chopped
- 1/4 cup shredded cheese (such as cheddar, mozzarella, or feta), optional
- Fresh herbs, chopped (such as parsley or chives), for garnish

Instructions:

1. **Prepare the filling:**
     - Heat a small non-stick skillet over medium heat. Add a teaspoon of butter or olive oil.
     - Add the sliced mushrooms to the skillet and sauté for 3-4 minutes, until they begin to soften and brown slightly.
2. **Add spinach:**
     - Add the chopped spinach leaves to the skillet with the mushrooms. Cook for another 1-2 minutes, stirring occasionally, until the spinach is wilted. Season with salt and pepper to taste. Remove from heat and set aside.
3. **Whisk the eggs:**
     - In a bowl, whisk together the eggs and milk (or water) until well combined. Season with a pinch of salt and pepper.
4. **Cook the omelette:**
     - Heat another non-stick skillet (about 8-10 inches in diameter) over medium heat. Add the remaining butter or olive oil and swirl to coat the pan evenly.
     - Pour the whisked eggs into the skillet. Let them cook undisturbed for about 1 minute, allowing the edges to set.
5. **Add the filling:**
     - Spoon the sautéed mushroom and spinach mixture evenly over one half of the omelette.
     - If using cheese, sprinkle it over the filling.
6. **Fold and finish cooking:**
     - Using a spatula, gently fold the other half of the omelette over the filling. Press down lightly with the spatula to seal.
     - Cook for another 1-2 minutes, or until the eggs are fully set and the cheese is melted (if using).
7. **Serve:**
     - Slide the spinach and mushroom omelette onto a plate. Garnish with chopped fresh herbs, if desired.

- Serve hot with toast, a side of fresh fruit, or a small salad.

Tips:

- **Variations:** Customize your omelette with other vegetables like bell peppers, onions, or tomatoes. You can also add cooked bacon or ham for extra flavor.
- **Make it healthier:** Use egg whites instead of whole eggs or increase the ratio of vegetables to eggs.
- **Non-stick skillet:** Using a good quality non-stick skillet will make it easier to flip and fold the omelette without it sticking.

This spinach and mushroom omelette is a satisfying and versatile dish that can be enjoyed for breakfast, brunch, or even a quick dinner. It's a great way to start your day with a nutritious meal!

Mango and Avocado Salsa

Ingredients:

- 1 ripe mango, peeled, pitted, and diced
- 1 ripe avocado, peeled, pitted, and diced
- 1/4 cup red onion, finely chopped
- 1/4 cup fresh cilantro, chopped
- Juice of 1 lime
- 1 small jalapeño pepper, seeded and finely chopped (optional, for heat)
- Salt and pepper, to taste

Instructions:

1. **Prepare the ingredients:**
    - Dice the mango and avocado into small, bite-sized pieces. Finely chop the red onion, cilantro, and jalapeño pepper (if using).
2. **Combine ingredients:**
    - In a medium bowl, combine the diced mango, diced avocado, chopped red onion, chopped cilantro, and chopped jalapeño pepper (if using).
3. **Add lime juice and season:**
    - Squeeze the juice of one lime over the salsa ingredients.
    - Season with salt and pepper to taste.
4. **Mix gently:**
    - Gently toss all the ingredients together until well combined. Be careful not to mash the avocado pieces.
5. **Chill (optional):**
    - For best flavor, let the salsa chill in the refrigerator for at least 15-30 minutes before serving to allow the flavors to meld together.
6. **Serve:**
    - Serve mango and avocado salsa as a topping for grilled chicken, fish, or tacos.
    - Alternatively, serve with tortilla chips as a refreshing appetizer or snack.

Tips:

- **Customize:** You can add diced tomatoes, bell peppers, or cucumber for extra crunch and flavor.
- **Adjust heat:** Control the spiciness by adjusting the amount of jalapeño pepper you add. For a milder salsa, remove the seeds and membranes from the jalapeño before chopping.
- **Storage:** Store leftover salsa in an airtight container in the refrigerator for up to 2 days. The avocado may oxidize over time, but the lime juice helps to slow this process.

Enjoy this mango and avocado salsa for its vibrant colors, fresh flavors, and versatility! It's a perfect addition to your summer meals or anytime you want a taste of tropical goodness.

Broccoli and Cheese Stuffed Chicken

Ingredients:

- 4 boneless, skinless chicken breasts
- Salt and pepper, to taste
- 1 cup cooked broccoli florets, chopped
- 1 cup shredded cheddar cheese (or your favorite cheese)
- 1/4 cup mayonnaise
- 2 tablespoons grated Parmesan cheese
- 1 clove garlic, minced
- 1/2 teaspoon dried basil
- 1/2 teaspoon dried oregano
- 1/4 teaspoon paprika
- Olive oil, for drizzling

Instructions:

1. **Preheat the oven:**
   - Preheat your oven to 375°F (190°C). Lightly grease a baking dish with olive oil or non-stick cooking spray.
2. **Prepare the chicken breasts:**
   - Place each chicken breast between two pieces of plastic wrap or in a resealable plastic bag. Pound them to an even thickness of about 1/2 inch using a meat mallet or rolling pin. Season both sides with salt and pepper.
3. **Make the filling:**
   - In a bowl, combine the chopped cooked broccoli, shredded cheddar cheese, mayonnaise, grated Parmesan cheese, minced garlic, dried basil, dried oregano, and paprika. Mix well until everything is evenly combined.
4. **Stuff the chicken breasts:**
   - Spoon the broccoli and cheese mixture evenly onto one side of each chicken breast. Fold the other side over the filling, pressing down gently to seal.
5. **Secure with toothpicks (optional):**
   - If needed, secure the stuffed chicken breasts with toothpicks to keep the filling inside during cooking. Just remember to remove them before serving.
6. **Bake the chicken:**
   - Place the stuffed chicken breasts in the prepared baking dish. Drizzle each chicken breast with a little olive oil.
   - Bake in the preheated oven for 25-30 minutes, or until the chicken is cooked through and reaches an internal temperature of 165°F (75°C).
7. **Serve:**
   - Remove the chicken from the oven and let it rest for a few minutes before serving.

- Serve the broccoli and cheese stuffed chicken hot, garnished with fresh herbs if desired.

Tips:

- **Variations:** Feel free to customize the filling with different cheeses like mozzarella or Monterey Jack, and add extras like chopped sun-dried tomatoes or spinach.
- **Side dish ideas:** Serve the stuffed chicken with a side of roasted vegetables, mashed potatoes, or a fresh green salad.
- **Make ahead:** You can prepare the stuffed chicken breasts ahead of time and refrigerate them until ready to bake. Increase the baking time slightly if cooking from chilled.

This broccoli and cheese stuffed chicken is sure to be a hit with its cheesy, flavorful filling and juicy chicken. It's perfect for a satisfying dinner that's both comforting and delicious!

Brown Rice and Lentil Pilaf

Ingredients:

- 1 cup brown rice
- 1/2 cup brown or green lentils
- 2 tablespoons olive oil or butter
- 1 onion, finely chopped
- 2 cloves garlic, minced
- 1 carrot, diced
- 1 celery stalk, diced
- 1 teaspoon ground cumin
- 1/2 teaspoon ground coriander
- 1/2 teaspoon ground turmeric
- 1/4 teaspoon ground cinnamon
- Salt and pepper, to taste
- 2 1/2 cups vegetable broth or chicken broth
- Optional garnish: Chopped fresh parsley or cilantro

Instructions:

1. **Prepare the rice and lentils:**
    - Rinse the brown rice and lentils separately under cold water until the water runs clear.
    - In a medium saucepan, combine the brown rice and lentils with 2 1/2 cups of vegetable broth or chicken broth. Bring to a boil over medium-high heat.
2. **Simmer the rice and lentils:**
    - Once boiling, reduce the heat to low and cover the saucepan. Let simmer for about 30-40 minutes, or until the rice and lentils are tender and the liquid is absorbed. Remove from heat and let it sit covered for 5-10 minutes.
3. **Prepare the vegetables:**
    - While the rice and lentils are cooking, heat olive oil or butter in a large skillet over medium heat.
    - Add the chopped onion and cook until softened and translucent, about 5-7 minutes.
    - Add the minced garlic, diced carrot, and diced celery to the skillet. Cook for another 3-4 minutes, stirring occasionally, until the vegetables are tender.
4. **Add spices:**
    - Stir in the ground cumin, ground coriander, ground turmeric, ground cinnamon, salt, and pepper. Cook for 1 minute, stirring constantly, until the spices are fragrant.
5. **Combine rice, lentils, and vegetables:**
    - Add the cooked rice and lentils to the skillet with the sautéed vegetables. Stir well to combine and coat the rice and lentils with the spices and vegetables.

6. **Finish and serve:**
    - Taste and adjust seasoning if needed. Serve the brown rice and lentil pilaf warm, garnished with chopped fresh parsley or cilantro if desired.

Tips:

- **Variations:** You can add other vegetables like bell peppers, peas, or spinach to the pilaf for added texture and flavor.
- **Protein options:** Serve the pilaf with grilled chicken, tofu, or chickpeas for a complete meal.
- **Storage:** Leftover pilaf can be stored in an airtight container in the refrigerator for up to 3-4 days. Reheat gently in the microwave or on the stovetop with a splash of broth to refresh.

This Brown Rice and Lentil Pilaf is not only nutritious but also full of comforting flavors. It makes a satisfying main dish or a delicious side alongside your favorite protein. Enjoy the wholesome goodness of this hearty pilaf!

Grilled Shrimp Skewers

Ingredients:

- 1 pound large shrimp, peeled and deveined
- 2 tablespoons olive oil
- 2 cloves garlic, minced
- 1 teaspoon paprika
- 1/2 teaspoon ground cumin
- 1/2 teaspoon ground coriander
- 1/4 teaspoon cayenne pepper (optional, for heat)
- Salt and pepper, to taste
- 1 lemon, juiced
- Wooden or metal skewers

Instructions:

1. **Prepare the shrimp:**
   - If using wooden skewers, soak them in water for at least 30 minutes to prevent burning while grilling.
   - In a large bowl, combine the olive oil, minced garlic, paprika, ground cumin, ground coriander, cayenne pepper (if using), salt, pepper, and lemon juice. Mix well to combine.
2. **Marinate the shrimp:**
   - Add the peeled and deveined shrimp to the marinade. Toss to coat evenly. Cover the bowl with plastic wrap and refrigerate for at least 15-30 minutes to allow the flavors to meld.
3. **Skewer the shrimp:**
   - Preheat your grill to medium-high heat.
   - Thread the marinated shrimp onto skewers, leaving a little space between each shrimp.
4. **Grill the skewers:**
   - Place the shrimp skewers on the preheated grill. Cook for 2-3 minutes per side, or until the shrimp are opaque and slightly charred.
   - Avoid overcooking the shrimp, as they can become rubbery. Shrimp cook quickly, so keep an eye on them.
5. **Serve:**
   - Once cooked through, remove the shrimp skewers from the grill.
   - Serve the grilled shrimp skewers hot, garnished with additional lemon wedges and fresh herbs if desired.

Tips:

- **Variations:** You can customize the marinade by adding herbs like chopped fresh parsley or cilantro, or using different spices such as smoked paprika or chili powder.
- **Side dishes:** Grilled shrimp skewers pair well with a variety of sides, such as rice pilaf, grilled vegetables, or a fresh green salad.
- **Preparation:** If using wooden skewers, remember to soak them in water beforehand to prevent them from burning on the grill.

Grilled shrimp skewers are quick to prepare and packed with flavor, making them a fantastic choice for a light and satisfying meal. Enjoy the juicy and tender shrimp with your favorite sides for a delightful dining experience!

Greek Salad with Feta Cheese

Ingredients:

- 2 cups cherry tomatoes, halved
- 1 cucumber, diced
- 1 red bell pepper, diced
- 1/2 red onion, thinly sliced
- 1/2 cup Kalamata olives, pitted
- 1/2 cup crumbled feta cheese
- 1/4 cup extra virgin olive oil
- 2 tablespoons red wine vinegar
- 1 teaspoon dried oregano
- Salt and pepper, to taste
- Fresh parsley or basil leaves, chopped (optional, for garnish)

Instructions:

1. **Prepare the vegetables:**
   - In a large salad bowl, combine the cherry tomatoes, diced cucumber, diced red bell pepper, thinly sliced red onion, and Kalamata olives.
2. **Make the dressing:**
   - In a small bowl or jar, whisk together the extra virgin olive oil, red wine vinegar, dried oregano, salt, and pepper. Adjust seasoning to taste.
3. **Assemble the salad:**
   - Pour the dressing over the salad ingredients in the bowl. Toss gently to coat all the vegetables with the dressing.
4. **Add feta cheese:**
   - Sprinkle the crumbled feta cheese over the salad.
5. **Garnish and serve:**
   - If desired, garnish the Greek salad with chopped fresh parsley or basil leaves for added freshness and color.
6. **Serve immediately:**
   - Serve the Greek salad immediately as a side dish or as a light main course.

Tips:

- **Variations:** You can add other ingredients like sliced cucumbers, pepperoncini peppers, or even grilled chicken or shrimp for added protein.
- **Make ahead:** You can prepare the vegetables and dressing ahead of time but wait to add the feta cheese until just before serving to keep it fresh.
- **Storage:** Leftover Greek salad can be stored in an airtight container in the refrigerator for up to 2 days. The flavors will continue to meld together over time.

This Greek salad with feta cheese is refreshing, flavorful, and perfect for any occasion. Enjoy its vibrant colors and Mediterranean-inspired taste as part of a balanced meal or as a light and satisfying snack!

Baked Eggplant Parmesan

Ingredients:

- 2 medium eggplants, sliced into 1/2-inch rounds
- Salt, for sweating the eggplant
- 1 cup all-purpose flour
- 3 large eggs, beaten
- 2 cups Italian-style breadcrumbs
- 1/2 cup grated Parmesan cheese
- 2 cups marinara sauce (homemade or store-bought)
- 2 cups shredded mozzarella cheese
- Fresh basil leaves, chopped, for garnish (optional)
- Olive oil cooking spray

Instructions:

1. **Prepare the eggplant:**
    - Preheat your oven to 400°F (200°C). Line a baking sheet with parchment paper.
    - Place the eggplant slices on a large baking sheet or tray in a single layer. Sprinkle both sides of each slice generously with salt. Let them sit for about 20 minutes to draw out excess moisture. Pat dry with paper towels.
2. **Set up the breading station:**
    - Prepare three shallow bowls or dishes. Place the flour in the first bowl, beaten eggs in the second bowl, and breadcrumbs mixed with grated Parmesan cheese in the third bowl.
3. **Bread the eggplant slices:**
    - Dredge each eggplant slice in the flour, shaking off any excess.
    - Dip the floured slice into the beaten eggs, allowing any excess to drip off.
    - Coat the eggplant slice thoroughly with the breadcrumb mixture, pressing gently to adhere. Place the breaded slices on the prepared baking sheet.
4. **Bake the eggplant:**
    - Lightly spray the tops of the breaded eggplant slices with olive oil cooking spray.
    - Bake in the preheated oven for 20-25 minutes, flipping halfway through, until the eggplant slices are golden brown and crispy. Remove from the oven and reduce the oven temperature to 350°F (175°C).
5. **Assemble the Eggplant Parmesan:**
    - Spread a thin layer of marinara sauce on the bottom of a 9x13-inch baking dish.
    - Arrange half of the baked eggplant slices in a single layer over the sauce.
    - Spoon half of the remaining marinara sauce evenly over the eggplant slices.
    - Sprinkle half of the shredded mozzarella cheese over the sauce.
    - Repeat the layers with the remaining eggplant slices, marinara sauce, and shredded mozzarella cheese.
6. **Bake:**

- Cover the baking dish with aluminum foil and bake in the 350°F (175°C) oven for 20 minutes.
- Remove the foil and bake for an additional 10-15 minutes, or until the cheese is melted and bubbly.

7. **Serve:**
   - Remove from the oven and let the Baked Eggplant Parmesan rest for a few minutes before serving.
   - Garnish with chopped fresh basil leaves, if desired, before serving.

Tips:

- **Make it gluten-free:** Use gluten-free breadcrumbs and flour to make this dish gluten-free.
- **Variations:** Add a layer of ricotta cheese or fresh basil leaves between the layers for extra flavor.
- **Storage:** Leftovers can be stored in an airtight container in the refrigerator for up to 3 days. Reheat in the oven or microwave until heated through.

Enjoy this Baked Eggplant Parmesan as a hearty and satisfying main dish. It's perfect served with a side of pasta or a fresh green salad for a complete meal!

Chicken and Vegetable Curry

Ingredients:

- 1 pound boneless, skinless chicken breasts or thighs, cut into bite-sized pieces
- 2 tablespoons vegetable oil or ghee
- 1 onion, finely chopped
- 3 cloves garlic, minced
- 1 tablespoon fresh ginger, grated or minced
- 1 red bell pepper, sliced
- 1 zucchini, sliced
- 1 cup cauliflower florets
- 1 cup green beans, trimmed and cut into bite-sized pieces
- 1 carrot, sliced
- 1 tablespoon curry powder
- 1 teaspoon ground cumin
- 1 teaspoon ground coriander
- 1/2 teaspoon turmeric powder
- 1/4 teaspoon cayenne pepper (adjust to taste)
- 1 can (14 ounces) coconut milk
- 1 cup chicken broth
- Salt and pepper, to taste
- Fresh cilantro, chopped, for garnish
- Cooked rice or naan bread, for serving

Instructions:

1. **Prepare the chicken and vegetables:**
    - Heat vegetable oil or ghee in a large skillet or Dutch oven over medium-high heat. Add the chopped onion and sauté until softened, about 3-4 minutes.
    - Add minced garlic and grated ginger to the skillet. Cook for another minute until fragrant.
2. **Cook the chicken:**
    - Add the chicken pieces to the skillet. Cook, stirring occasionally, until the chicken is browned on all sides, about 5-6 minutes.
3. **Add spices:**
    - Sprinkle curry powder, ground cumin, ground coriander, turmeric powder, and cayenne pepper over the chicken and vegetables. Stir well to coat the chicken evenly with the spices.
4. **Add vegetables:**
    - Add the sliced red bell pepper, zucchini, cauliflower florets, green beans, and carrot to the skillet. Stir to combine with the chicken and spices.
5. **Simmer the curry:**

- Pour in the coconut milk and chicken broth. Stir well to combine all the ingredients. Bring the mixture to a boil, then reduce the heat to low. Cover and simmer for 15-20 minutes, or until the chicken is cooked through and the vegetables are tender.

6. **Adjust seasoning:**
    - Taste and season with salt and pepper as needed. Adjust the level of cayenne pepper for spiciness according to your preference.
7. **Serve:**
    - Serve the chicken and vegetable curry hot, garnished with chopped fresh cilantro. Serve over cooked rice or with naan bread on the side.

Tips:

- **Vegetable variations:** Feel free to customize the vegetables based on what you have on hand or prefer. Other options include spinach, peas, potatoes, or eggplant.
- **Coconut milk:** Use full-fat coconut milk for a creamier and richer curry sauce. Shake the can well before opening to incorporate the cream with the milk.
- **Storage:** Leftover curry can be stored in an airtight container in the refrigerator for up to 3-4 days. Reheat gently on the stovetop or in the microwave.

Enjoy this flavorful chicken and vegetable curry as a satisfying meal that's perfect for dinner any day of the week. It's sure to warm you up with its aromatic spices and creamy coconut milk base!

Kale and Berry Smoothie

Ingredients:

- 1 cup fresh kale leaves, chopped
- 1/2 cup mixed berries (such as strawberries, blueberries, raspberries)
- 1 banana, peeled and sliced
- 1 tablespoon chia seeds
- 1 tablespoon honey or maple syrup (optional, for sweetness)
- 1 cup almond milk or any milk of your choice
- Ice cubes (optional, for a chilled smoothie)

Instructions:

1. **Prepare the kale and berries:**
   - Rinse the kale leaves thoroughly and chop them into smaller pieces.
2. **Combine ingredients:**
   - In a blender, add the chopped kale leaves, mixed berries, sliced banana, chia seeds, honey or maple syrup (if using), and almond milk.
3. **Blend until smooth:**
   - Blend on high speed until all ingredients are well combined and the smoothie reaches a creamy consistency. If desired, add ice cubes and blend again until smooth.
4. **Adjust consistency:**
   - If the smoothie is too thick, add more almond milk or water to reach your desired consistency.
5. **Serve:**
   - Pour the Kale and Berry Smoothie into glasses. Optionally, garnish with additional berries or a sprinkle of chia seeds on top.

Tips:

- **Variations:** Feel free to customize your smoothie by adding other ingredients such as spinach, avocado, Greek yogurt, or protein powder for added nutrition.
- **Sweetness:** Adjust the sweetness level by adding more or less honey or maple syrup, depending on your taste preferences.
- **Make it ahead:** Prepare smoothie packs by portioning out the kale, berries, banana, and chia seeds into freezer-safe bags. When ready to make a smoothie, simply dump the contents of the bag into the blender with almond milk and blend.

This Kale and Berry Smoothie is packed with vitamins, antioxidants, and fiber from the kale and berries, making it a nutritious and delicious choice for a quick breakfast or refreshing snack. Enjoy its vibrant color and refreshing taste!

Roasted Brussels Sprouts with Balsamic Glaze

Ingredients:

- 1 pound Brussels sprouts, trimmed and halved
- 2 tablespoons olive oil
- Salt and pepper, to taste
- 2-3 tablespoons balsamic glaze or balsamic reduction

Instructions:

1. **Preheat the oven:**
   - Preheat your oven to 400°F (200°C).
2. **Prepare the Brussels sprouts:**
   - Trim the ends of the Brussels sprouts and cut them in half lengthwise. Remove any outer leaves that are yellow or damaged.
3. **Toss with olive oil and seasonings:**
   - Place the halved Brussels sprouts on a large baking sheet. Drizzle with olive oil and season with salt and pepper. Toss well to coat evenly.
4. **Roast in the oven:**
   - Arrange the Brussels sprouts in a single layer on the baking sheet, cut side down if possible.
   - Roast in the preheated oven for 20-25 minutes, or until the Brussels sprouts are golden brown and crispy on the edges, stirring halfway through cooking for even browning.
5. **Finish with balsamic glaze:**
   - Remove the Brussels sprouts from the oven and transfer them to a serving dish.
   - Drizzle the roasted Brussels sprouts with balsamic glaze or balsamic reduction. Toss gently to coat the sprouts with the glaze.
6. **Serve:**
   - Transfer the roasted Brussels sprouts with balsamic glaze to a serving platter. Optionally, garnish with a sprinkle of freshly cracked black pepper or grated Parmesan cheese.

Tips:

- **Balsamic glaze:** If you don't have store-bought balsamic glaze, you can make your own by simmering balsamic vinegar in a saucepan over medium heat until it reduces and thickens into a syrupy consistency.
- **Variations:** Add crispy cooked bacon or toasted nuts (such as walnuts or almonds) for added texture and flavor.
- **Storage:** Roasted Brussels sprouts are best enjoyed fresh but can be stored in an airtight container in the refrigerator for up to 2 days. Reheat gently in the oven or microwave before serving.

This roasted Brussels sprouts with balsamic glaze recipe makes a fantastic side dish for any meal, offering a perfect balance of sweet and savory flavors. Enjoy the crispy edges and tender centers of the Brussels sprouts enhanced by the tangy balsamic glaze!

Whole Wheat Banana Pancakes

Ingredients:

- 1 cup whole wheat flour
- 1 tablespoon baking powder
- 1/4 teaspoon salt
- 1 tablespoon honey or maple syrup (optional, for sweetness)
- 1 cup milk (dairy or plant-based)
- 1 ripe banana, mashed
- 1 large egg
- 2 tablespoons melted butter or vegetable oil
- 1 teaspoon vanilla extract
- Butter or oil, for cooking

Instructions:

1. **Prepare the batter:**
   - In a large bowl, whisk together the whole wheat flour, baking powder, and salt.
2. **Mix wet ingredients:**
   - In another bowl, mash the ripe banana using a fork until smooth. Add the honey or maple syrup (if using), milk, egg, melted butter or oil, and vanilla extract. Stir well to combine.
3. **Combine wet and dry ingredients:**
   - Pour the wet ingredients into the bowl with the dry ingredients. Stir gently until just combined. Be careful not to overmix; a few lumps are okay.
4. **Heat the griddle or skillet:**
   - Heat a non-stick griddle or skillet over medium heat. Lightly grease the surface with butter or oil.
5. **Cook the pancakes:**
   - Pour about 1/4 cup of batter onto the heated griddle for each pancake. Use the back of a spoon or ladle to spread the batter into a circle, if needed.
   - Cook until bubbles form on the surface of the pancake and the edges look set, about 2-3 minutes.
6. **Flip and cook the other side:**
   - Carefully flip the pancake with a spatula and cook for another 1-2 minutes, or until golden brown and cooked through.
7. **Serve:**
   - Transfer the cooked pancakes to a plate and keep warm while you cook the remaining pancakes.
   - Serve the Whole Wheat Banana Pancakes warm, topped with sliced bananas, a drizzle of honey or maple syrup, and a sprinkle of chopped nuts or berries if desired.

Tips:

- **Ripe bananas:** The riper the banana, the sweeter and more flavorful your pancakes will be.
- **Variations:** Add a pinch of cinnamon or nutmeg to the batter for extra warmth and flavor.
- **Storage:** Leftover pancakes can be stored in an airtight container in the refrigerator for up to 2 days. Reheat in the toaster or microwave before serving.

These Whole Wheat Banana Pancakes are not only wholesome but also easy to make, perfect for a satisfying breakfast or brunch. Enjoy their fluffy texture and natural sweetness from the bananas!

Zucchini Noodles with Pesto

Ingredients:

- 3 medium zucchinis
- 1/2 cup homemade or store-bought pesto sauce
- 1 tablespoon olive oil
- Salt and pepper, to taste
- Grated Parmesan cheese, for garnish (optional)
- Cherry tomatoes, halved, for garnish (optional)
- Toasted pine nuts or chopped walnuts, for garnish (optional)

Instructions:

1. **Prepare the zucchini noodles:**
   - Wash the zucchinis thoroughly. Trim off the ends.
   - Use a spiralizer to create zucchini noodles (zoodles). Alternatively, you can use a vegetable peeler to create long, thin strips resembling noodles.
2. **Cook the zucchini noodles:**
   - Heat olive oil in a large skillet over medium-high heat.
   - Add the zucchini noodles to the skillet. Cook for 2-3 minutes, tossing gently with tongs, until the zoodles are just tender but still crisp. Be careful not to overcook them, as they can become mushy.
3. **Combine with pesto sauce:**
   - Reduce the heat to low. Add the pesto sauce to the skillet with the zucchini noodles. Toss well to coat the noodles evenly with the pesto sauce. Heat through for about 1 minute.
4. **Season and garnish:**
   - Season with salt and pepper to taste.
   - Optionally, garnish the zucchini noodles with grated Parmesan cheese, halved cherry tomatoes, and toasted pine nuts or chopped walnuts for added texture and flavor.
5. **Serve:**
   - Divide the zucchini noodles with pesto among serving plates or bowls.
   - Enjoy immediately as a light and nutritious meal on its own, or serve as a side dish with grilled chicken, shrimp, or fish.

Tips:

- **Variations:** Feel free to add grilled chicken, shrimp, or tofu for added protein. You can also mix in sun-dried tomatoes or roasted vegetables for extra flavor.
- **Storage:** Zucchini noodles are best enjoyed fresh but can be stored in an airtight container in the refrigerator for up to 2 days. Reheat gently in a skillet or microwave before serving.

This zucchini noodles with pesto recipe is a great way to enjoy a low-carb, gluten-free alternative to pasta while still savoring the flavors of pesto sauce and fresh zucchini. It's quick to prepare and makes a perfect light meal or side dish!

Black Bean and Corn Salad

Ingredients:

- 1 can (15 ounces) black beans, drained and rinsed
- 1 cup corn kernels (fresh, canned, or frozen)
- 1 red bell pepper, diced
- 1/2 red onion, finely chopped
- 1 jalapeño pepper, seeded and finely chopped (optional, for heat)
- 1/4 cup chopped fresh cilantro
- Juice of 1 lime
- 2 tablespoons olive oil
- 1 teaspoon ground cumin
- 1/2 teaspoon chili powder
- Salt and pepper, to taste
- Optional: Avocado, diced, for extra creaminess

Instructions:

1. **Prepare the Dressing:**
   - In a small bowl, whisk together the lime juice, olive oil, ground cumin, chili powder, salt, and pepper. Set aside.
2. **Combine Ingredients:**
   - In a large mixing bowl, combine the black beans, corn kernels, diced red bell pepper, finely chopped red onion, chopped jalapeño (if using), and chopped cilantro.
3. **Add Dressing:**
   - Pour the dressing over the salad ingredients in the bowl.
4. **Mix Gently:**
   - Gently toss everything together until well combined and evenly coated with the dressing. If you're adding diced avocado, gently fold it in at this stage.
5. **Chill (Optional):**
   - For best flavor, you can chill the salad in the refrigerator for about 30 minutes to let the flavors meld together before serving.
6. **Serve:**
   - Serve the black bean and corn salad chilled or at room temperature.

Tips:

- **Variations:** Feel free to add other ingredients such as cherry tomatoes, diced cucumber, or chopped green onions.
- **Storage:** Store any leftover salad in an airtight container in the refrigerator for up to 3-4 days. The flavors will continue to develop over time.

- **Serve Creatively:** This salad is versatile and can be served as a side dish, on top of grilled chicken or fish, or as a filling for tacos or wraps.

This black bean and corn salad is not only colorful and flavorful but also nutritious, packed with protein, fiber, and essential vitamins. It's a perfect dish for picnics, potlucks, or any occasion where you want a fresh and healthy option!

Salmon and Asparagus Foil Packets

Ingredients:

- 4 salmon fillets (about 6 ounces each)
- 1 bunch asparagus, trimmed
- 2 tablespoons olive oil
- 4 cloves garlic, minced
- 1 lemon, thinly sliced
- Salt and pepper, to taste
- Fresh herbs (such as dill, parsley, or thyme), for garnish
- Optional: Red pepper flakes, for a hint of spice

Instructions:

1. **Preheat the Oven:**
   - Preheat your oven to 400°F (200°C).
2. **Prepare Foil Packets:**
   - Tear off 4 large pieces of aluminum foil, each about 12 inches long.
   - Place one salmon fillet in the center of each piece of foil.
3. **Season Salmon:**
   - Drizzle olive oil over each salmon fillet.
   - Sprinkle minced garlic evenly over the salmon.
   - Season with salt and pepper to taste.
4. **Add Asparagus and Lemon:**
   - Divide the trimmed asparagus evenly among the foil packets, arranging them around the salmon fillets.
   - Place a couple of lemon slices on top of each salmon fillet.
5. **Fold Foil Packets:**
   - Fold the sides of the foil over the salmon and asparagus, covering completely.
   - Seal the edges tightly to create closed packets. Make sure there is some room inside for steam to circulate.
6. **Bake in the Oven:**
   - Place the foil packets on a baking sheet and bake in the preheated oven for 15-20 minutes, depending on the thickness of the salmon fillets. The salmon should flake easily with a fork when done.
7. **Serve:**
   - Carefully open the foil packets (watch out for steam) and transfer the salmon and asparagus to plates.
   - Garnish with fresh herbs and red pepper flakes, if desired.
   - Serve hot with a side of rice, quinoa, or a fresh green salad.

Tips:

- **Variations:** You can customize the seasoning by adding spices like paprika, cumin, or herbs like rosemary or thyme.
- **Grilling Option:** These foil packets can also be cooked on the grill over medium-high heat for about 10-12 minutes. Make sure to flip them halfway through cooking.
- **Ingredient Substitutions:** If you prefer, you can substitute the asparagus with other vegetables like green beans, zucchini, or cherry tomatoes.

These salmon and asparagus foil packets are not only flavorful and healthy but also make cleanup a breeze. Enjoy this simple yet satisfying meal that's perfect for busy weeknights or weekend dinners!

Quinoa and Black Bean Stuffed Peppers

Ingredients:

- 4 large bell peppers (any color), tops cut off and seeds removed
- 1 cup quinoa, rinsed
- 1 can (15 ounces) black beans, drained and rinsed
- 1 cup corn kernels (fresh, canned, or frozen)
- 1/2 onion, diced
- 2 cloves garlic, minced
- 1 teaspoon ground cumin
- 1 teaspoon chili powder
- 1/2 teaspoon paprika
- Salt and pepper, to taste
- 1 cup shredded cheese (such as cheddar or Monterey Jack), divided
- Fresh cilantro or parsley, chopped, for garnish
- Optional toppings: salsa, sour cream, avocado slices

Instructions:

1. **Preheat the Oven:**
   - Preheat your oven to 375°F (190°C). Lightly grease a baking dish large enough to hold the bell peppers upright.
2. **Prepare the Quinoa:**
   - In a medium saucepan, bring 2 cups of water to a boil. Add the quinoa, reduce heat to low, cover, and simmer for about 15 minutes, or until the quinoa is cooked and water is absorbed. Remove from heat and let it sit covered for 5 minutes. Fluff with a fork.
3. **Prepare the Bell Peppers:**
   - While the quinoa is cooking, prepare the bell peppers. Cut off the tops and remove the seeds and membranes from inside the peppers. Rinse them under cold water.
4. **Make the Filling:**
   - In a large skillet, heat olive oil over medium heat. Add diced onion and cook until softened, about 5 minutes. Add minced garlic, ground cumin, chili powder, paprika, salt, and pepper. Cook for another 1-2 minutes until fragrant.
5. **Combine Ingredients:**
   - Add black beans and corn to the skillet. Stir in the cooked quinoa and 1/2 cup shredded cheese. Mix well until everything is combined and heated through. Adjust seasoning to taste.
6. **Stuff the Peppers:**
   - Place the prepared bell peppers upright in the greased baking dish. Spoon the quinoa and black bean mixture evenly into each pepper cavity. Press down gently to pack the filling.

7. **Bake the Stuffed Peppers:**
    - Cover the baking dish with foil and bake in the preheated oven for 30-35 minutes, or until the peppers are tender.
8. **Add Cheese and Finish:**
    - Remove the foil and sprinkle the remaining 1/2 cup of shredded cheese over the tops of the stuffed peppers. Return the dish to the oven and bake uncovered for an additional 5-10 minutes, or until the cheese is melted and bubbly.
9. **Serve:**
    - Remove the stuffed peppers from the oven. Garnish with chopped cilantro or parsley. Serve hot with optional toppings like salsa, sour cream, or avocado slices.

Tips:

- **Make Ahead:** You can prepare the filling ahead of time and store it in an airtight container in the refrigerator for up to 2 days. When ready to serve, stuff the peppers and bake.
- **Vegetarian/Vegan Options:** To make this dish vegan, omit the cheese or use a dairy-free cheese substitute. Ensure all other ingredients are vegan-friendly.
- **Variations:** Feel free to add diced tomatoes, spinach, or other vegetables to the quinoa and black bean mixture for extra flavor and nutrition.

These quinoa and black bean stuffed peppers are not only satisfying and flavorful but also packed with protein, fiber, and essential nutrients. They make a perfect main dish for a vegetarian dinner or a delicious side dish for any meal!

Turkey Meatballs with Marinara Sauce

Ingredients:

For the Turkey Meatballs:

- 1 pound ground turkey (preferably lean)
- 1/2 cup breadcrumbs (panko or regular)
- 1/4 cup grated Parmesan cheese
- 1/4 cup milk
- 1 egg, lightly beaten
- 2 cloves garlic, minced
- 2 tablespoons chopped fresh parsley (or 1 tablespoon dried parsley)
- 1 teaspoon dried oregano
- 1/2 teaspoon salt
- 1/4 teaspoon black pepper
- Olive oil, for cooking

For the Marinara Sauce:

- 2 tablespoons olive oil
- 1 onion, finely chopped
- 2 cloves garlic, minced
- 1 can (28 ounces) crushed tomatoes
- 1 teaspoon dried basil
- 1 teaspoon dried oregano
- 1/2 teaspoon dried thyme
- 1/2 teaspoon sugar (optional, to balance acidity)
- Salt and pepper, to taste

For Serving:

- Cooked pasta of your choice (spaghetti, fettuccine, etc.)
- Fresh basil leaves, chopped, for garnish
- Grated Parmesan cheese, for garnish

Instructions:

1. **Make the Turkey Meatballs:**
   - In a large mixing bowl, combine ground turkey, breadcrumbs, grated Parmesan cheese, milk, egg, minced garlic, chopped parsley, dried oregano, salt, and black pepper. Mix until well combined.
   - Shape the mixture into meatballs, about 1 to 1.5 inches in diameter. You should get approximately 20 meatballs from the mixture.

- In a large skillet, heat olive oil over medium-high heat. Add the meatballs in batches, making sure not to overcrowd the pan. Cook for about 3-4 minutes per side, or until browned and cooked through. Remove the cooked meatballs from the skillet and set aside.

2. **Make the Marinara Sauce:**
    - In the same skillet (or a separate saucepan), heat 2 tablespoons of olive oil over medium heat. Add finely chopped onion and cook until softened and translucent, about 5-6 minutes.
    - Add minced garlic and cook for another 1-2 minutes until fragrant.
    - Stir in crushed tomatoes, dried basil, dried oregano, dried thyme, and sugar (if using). Season with salt and pepper to taste.
    - Bring the sauce to a simmer. Reduce heat to low and let it simmer for 15-20 minutes, stirring occasionally, to allow the flavors to meld together.
3. **Combine Meatballs and Sauce:**
    - Add the cooked turkey meatballs to the marinara sauce, making sure they are coated evenly with the sauce.
    - Let the meatballs simmer in the sauce for an additional 5-10 minutes to absorb the flavors.
4. **Serve:**
    - Serve the turkey meatballs and marinara sauce over cooked pasta of your choice.
    - Garnish with chopped fresh basil leaves and grated Parmesan cheese.
    - Enjoy your delicious turkey meatballs with marinara sauce!

Tips:

- **Baking Option:** If you prefer a healthier cooking method, you can bake the meatballs in the oven at 400°F (200°C) for 15-20 minutes, or until cooked through.
- **Make Ahead:** You can prepare the meatballs and sauce ahead of time. Store them separately in the refrigerator and reheat gently before serving.
- **Variations:** Feel free to add crushed red pepper flakes for a spicy kick or incorporate chopped spinach or grated zucchini into the meatball mixture for added vegetables.

This turkey meatballs with marinara sauce recipe is sure to be a hit at the dinner table. It's hearty, flavorful, and perfect for serving with pasta or even on its own with a side of crusty bread. Enjoy!

Lentil and Vegetable Soup

Ingredients:

- 1 cup dried lentils (brown or green), rinsed and drained
- 1 tablespoon olive oil
- 1 onion, diced
- 2 carrots, diced
- 2 celery stalks, diced
- 3 cloves garlic, minced
- 1 teaspoon ground cumin
- 1 teaspoon ground coriander
- 1/2 teaspoon smoked paprika (optional, for a smoky flavor)
- 1/4 teaspoon red pepper flakes (optional, for heat)
- 1 can (14.5 ounces) diced tomatoes
- 4 cups vegetable broth (or chicken broth)
- 2 cups water
- 1 bay leaf
- Salt and pepper, to taste
- Fresh parsley or cilantro, chopped, for garnish
- Lemon wedges, for serving

Instructions:

1. **Prepare Lentils:**
   - Rinse the lentils under cold water and drain well.
2. **Sauté Vegetables:**
   - In a large pot or Dutch oven, heat olive oil over medium heat. Add diced onion, carrots, and celery. Cook, stirring occasionally, for about 5-7 minutes until vegetables begin to soften.
3. **Add Garlic and Spices:**
   - Add minced garlic, ground cumin, ground coriander, smoked paprika (if using), and red pepper flakes (if using). Cook for another 1-2 minutes until fragrant.
4. **Add Lentils and Liquid:**
   - Stir in the rinsed lentils, diced tomatoes (with their juices), vegetable broth, water, and bay leaf. Season with salt and pepper to taste.
5. **Simmer:**
   - Bring the soup to a boil, then reduce heat to low. Cover and let the soup simmer for about 25-30 minutes, or until the lentils and vegetables are tender.
6. **Adjust Seasoning:**
   - Taste and adjust seasoning as needed, adding more salt, pepper, or spices according to your preference.
7. **Serve:**
   - Remove the bay leaf from the soup.

- Ladle the lentil and vegetable soup into bowls. Garnish with chopped fresh parsley or cilantro.
- Serve with lemon wedges on the side for squeezing over the soup just before eating.

Tips:

- **Variations:** You can add other vegetables such as diced potatoes, bell peppers, or spinach to the soup for extra flavor and nutrition.
- **Texture:** For a thicker soup, blend a portion of the soup with an immersion blender or in a blender until smooth, then return it to the pot and heat through before serving.
- **Storage:** This soup keeps well in the refrigerator for up to 4-5 days. You may need to add a bit of water or broth when reheating as the lentils will absorb liquid over time.

This lentil and vegetable soup is not only delicious and comforting but also packed with protein, fiber, and essential nutrients. It's a perfect meal for lunch or dinner, especially when served with crusty bread or a side salad. Enjoy!

Baked Halibut with Lemon and Garlic

Ingredients:

- 4 halibut fillets (about 6 ounces each)
- Salt and pepper, to taste
- 2 tablespoons olive oil
- 4 cloves garlic, minced
- Zest of 1 lemon
- Juice of 1 lemon
- 1 tablespoon chopped fresh parsley (or 1 teaspoon dried parsley)
- 1/2 teaspoon dried thyme (or 1 tablespoon fresh thyme leaves)
- Lemon slices, for garnish
- Fresh parsley, chopped, for garnish

Instructions:

1. **Preheat the Oven:**
   - Preheat your oven to 400°F (200°C). Lightly grease a baking dish large enough to hold the halibut fillets in a single layer.
2. **Prepare the Halibut:**
   - Pat the halibut fillets dry with paper towels. Season both sides with salt and pepper.
3. **Make the Lemon Garlic Mixture:**
   - In a small bowl, combine olive oil, minced garlic, lemon zest, lemon juice, chopped parsley, and dried thyme (if using dried). Mix well to combine.
4. **Coat the Halibut:**
   - Place the halibut fillets in the prepared baking dish. Brush each fillet generously with the lemon garlic mixture, coating them evenly.
5. **Bake the Halibut:**
   - Bake in the preheated oven for 12-15 minutes, or until the halibut is opaque and flakes easily with a fork. The cooking time will depend on the thickness of your fillets, so adjust accordingly.
6. **Garnish and Serve:**
   - Remove the baked halibut from the oven. Garnish with lemon slices and chopped fresh parsley.
7. **Serve Immediately:**
   - Serve the baked halibut fillets hot, accompanied by your favorite sides such as steamed vegetables, rice, or a fresh green salad.

Tips:

- **Fresh Herbs:** If using fresh thyme, sprinkle it over the halibut fillets before baking instead of mixing it into the lemon garlic mixture.

- **Variations:** You can add a pinch of red pepper flakes or a dash of white wine to the lemon garlic mixture for extra flavor.
- **Checking Doneness:** Halibut is cooked through when it turns opaque and flakes easily with a fork. Be careful not to overcook it to keep it tender and juicy.

This baked halibut with lemon and garlic is a simple yet elegant dish that's perfect for a weeknight dinner or a special occasion. Enjoy the fresh flavors of lemon and herbs complementing the mild, flaky halibut!

Chickpea and Spinach Curry

Ingredients:

- 1 tablespoon vegetable oil
- 1 onion, finely chopped
- 3 cloves garlic, minced
- 1 tablespoon fresh ginger, minced (or 1 teaspoon ground ginger)
- 1 tablespoon curry powder
- 1 teaspoon ground cumin
- 1 teaspoon ground coriander
- 1/2 teaspoon turmeric powder
- 1/4 teaspoon cayenne pepper (adjust to taste, for heat)
- 1 can (15 ounces) chickpeas, drained and rinsed
- 1 can (14 ounces) diced tomatoes
- 1 can (14 ounces) coconut milk (full fat for creamier texture)
- 4 cups fresh spinach leaves, washed and chopped
- Salt and pepper, to taste
- Fresh cilantro, chopped, for garnish
- Cooked rice or naan bread, for serving

Instructions:

1. **Sauté Aromatics:**
   - Heat vegetable oil in a large skillet or pot over medium heat. Add chopped onion and cook until softened and translucent, about 5-7 minutes.
2. **Add Spices:**
   - Add minced garlic and fresh ginger (or ground ginger) to the skillet. Cook for another 1-2 minutes until fragrant.
3. **Toast Spices:**
   - Stir in curry powder, ground cumin, ground coriander, turmeric powder, and cayenne pepper (if using). Toast the spices for about 1 minute to enhance their flavors.
4. **Cook Chickpeas:**
   - Add drained and rinsed chickpeas to the skillet. Stir to coat them with the onion and spice mixture.
5. **Add Tomatoes and Coconut Milk:**
   - Pour in diced tomatoes (with their juices) and coconut milk. Stir well to combine all the ingredients.
6. **Simmer:**
   - Bring the mixture to a simmer. Reduce heat to low and let it simmer for about 10 minutes, stirring occasionally, to allow the flavors to meld together and the sauce to thicken slightly.
7. **Add Spinach:**

- Add chopped spinach leaves to the skillet. Stir until the spinach wilts and incorporates into the curry sauce, about 2-3 minutes.
8. **Season and Garnish:**
    - Season the chickpea and spinach curry with salt and pepper to taste. Adjust seasoning as needed.
9. **Serve:**
    - Remove from heat. Serve the chickpea and spinach curry hot over cooked rice or with naan bread.
10. **Garnish:**
    - Garnish with chopped fresh cilantro before serving for added freshness and flavor.

Tips:

- **Variations:** Feel free to add other vegetables such as diced bell peppers, peas, or carrots to the curry for extra texture and nutrition.
- **Creaminess:** For a richer curry, you can stir in a tablespoon of creamy peanut butter or a dollop of plain yogurt towards the end of cooking.
- **Storage:** Leftovers can be stored in an airtight container in the refrigerator for up to 3-4 days. The flavors will continue to develop over time.

This chickpea and spinach curry is not only delicious and satisfying but also packed with protein, fiber, and essential nutrients. It's a perfect dish for a meatless meal that's both hearty and flavorful!

Whole Wheat Berry Muffins

Ingredients:

- 1 cup whole wheat flour
- 1 cup all-purpose flour
- 1/2 cup packed brown sugar (or granulated sugar)
- 1 tablespoon baking powder
- 1/2 teaspoon baking soda
- 1/2 teaspoon salt
- 1 cup plain yogurt (Greek yogurt or regular)
- 1/2 cup milk (any type: dairy or plant-based)
- 1/4 cup vegetable oil or melted butter
- 2 large eggs
- 1 teaspoon vanilla extract
- 1 cup fresh or frozen berries (such as blueberries, raspberries, or a mix)

Instructions:

1. **Preheat the Oven:**
   - Preheat your oven to 375°F (190°C). Line a muffin tin with paper liners or grease the muffin cups with cooking spray.
2. **Prepare Dry Ingredients:**
   - In a large bowl, whisk together whole wheat flour, all-purpose flour, brown sugar, baking powder, baking soda, and salt until well combined.
3. **Prepare Wet Ingredients:**
   - In another bowl, whisk together yogurt, milk, vegetable oil or melted butter, eggs, and vanilla extract until smooth.
4. **Combine Wet and Dry Ingredients:**
   - Pour the wet ingredients into the bowl with the dry ingredients. Stir gently with a wooden spoon or spatula until just combined. Do not overmix; a few lumps are okay.
5. **Add Berries:**
   - Gently fold in the berries into the muffin batter. If using frozen berries, do not thaw them beforehand to prevent excessive bleeding into the batter.
6. **Fill Muffin Cups:**
   - Divide the batter evenly among the prepared muffin cups, filling each about 2/3 full.
7. **Bake:**
   - Bake in the preheated oven for 18-20 minutes, or until the tops of the muffins are golden brown and a toothpick inserted into the center comes out clean.
8. **Cool and Serve:**
   - Remove the muffin tin from the oven and let the muffins cool in the tin for 5 minutes. Then, transfer them to a wire rack to cool completely.

9. **Enjoy:**
    - Serve the whole wheat berry muffins warm or at room temperature. They can be stored in an airtight container at room temperature for up to 3 days or frozen for longer storage.

Tips:

- **Berry Options:** You can use a single type of berry or a combination of berries according to your preference.
- **Whole Wheat Flour:** Using a mixture of whole wheat and all-purpose flour helps achieve a balance of flavor and texture.
- **Customization:** Feel free to add nuts, seeds, or a sprinkle of oats on top of the muffins before baking for added texture and nutrition.

These whole wheat berry muffins are perfect for breakfast, brunch, or as a snack any time of the day. They're moist, tender, and packed with fruity goodness, making them a hit with both kids and adults alike!

Caprese Salad with Balsamic Reduction

Ingredients:

- 2 large tomatoes, sliced into 1/4-inch rounds
- 1 ball (about 8 ounces) fresh mozzarella cheese, sliced into 1/4-inch rounds
- Fresh basil leaves
- Salt and pepper, to taste
- Extra virgin olive oil, for drizzling
- **For the Balsamic Reduction:**
    - 1/2 cup balsamic vinegar
    - 1 tablespoon honey or maple syrup (optional, for sweetness)

Instructions:

1. **Make the Balsamic Reduction:**
    - In a small saucepan, combine balsamic vinegar and honey or maple syrup (if using). Bring to a gentle boil over medium heat.
    - Reduce the heat to low and simmer, stirring occasionally, until the vinegar has thickened and reduced by half. This will take about 10-15 minutes. Remove from heat and let it cool slightly. The reduction will thicken further as it cools.
2. **Assemble the Salad:**
    - Arrange tomato slices and mozzarella slices alternately on a serving platter or individual plates, overlapping them slightly.
    - Tuck fresh basil leaves between the tomato and mozzarella slices.
3. **Season and Drizzle:**
    - Season the Caprese salad with salt and pepper to taste.
    - Drizzle extra virgin olive oil over the tomato and mozzarella slices.
4. **Drizzle with Balsamic Reduction:**
    - Spoon the balsamic reduction over the Caprese salad, focusing on the tomato and mozzarella slices.
5. **Serve:**
    - Serve the Caprese salad with balsamic reduction immediately, garnished with extra basil leaves if desired.

Tips:

- **Tomatoes and Mozzarella:** Use ripe, juicy tomatoes and fresh mozzarella cheese for the best flavor and texture.
- **Basil:** Fresh basil adds a fragrant and herbaceous flavor to the salad. You can tear the leaves or leave them whole.
- **Presentation:** Arrange the tomato and mozzarella slices in a circular pattern on a large platter for an attractive presentation.

- **Variations:** Add a drizzle of pesto sauce or sprinkle with pine nuts for extra flavor and texture.

This Caprese salad with balsamic reduction is a delightful appetizer or side dish that showcases the simplicity and freshness of Italian flavors. It's perfect for summer gatherings or anytime you want to enjoy a taste of Mediterranean cuisine!

Turkey and Vegetable Skewers

Ingredients:

- 1 pound turkey breast, cut into 1-inch cubes
- 1 red bell pepper, cut into chunks
- 1 yellow bell pepper, cut into chunks
- 1 red onion, cut into chunks
- 1 zucchini, sliced into rounds
- 8-10 cherry tomatoes
- 2 tablespoons olive oil
- 2 cloves garlic, minced
- 1 teaspoon dried oregano
- 1 teaspoon dried thyme
- 1 teaspoon paprika
- Salt and pepper, to taste
- Wooden or metal skewers

Instructions:

1. **Prepare the Marinade:**
   - In a small bowl, combine olive oil, minced garlic, dried oregano, dried thyme, paprika, salt, and pepper. Mix well to make the marinade.
2. **Marinate the Turkey:**
   - Place the turkey cubes in a shallow dish or a large resealable plastic bag. Pour the marinade over the turkey, making sure each piece is coated evenly. Marinate in the refrigerator for at least 30 minutes, or up to 2 hours for maximum flavor.
3. **Prepare the Skewers:**
   - If using wooden skewers, soak them in water for at least 30 minutes to prevent them from burning during cooking.
   - Preheat the grill or oven to medium-high heat.
4. **Assemble the Skewers:**
   - Thread the marinated turkey cubes and vegetables onto the skewers, alternating between turkey, bell peppers, onion, zucchini, and cherry tomatoes.
5. **Grill or Bake:**
   - Grill the skewers over medium-high heat for about 10-12 minutes, turning occasionally, until the turkey is cooked through and the vegetables are tender and lightly charred.
   - If baking, preheat the oven to 400°F (200°C). Place the skewers on a baking sheet lined with parchment paper or aluminum foil. Bake for 15-20 minutes, or until the turkey is cooked through and the vegetables are tender.
6. **Serve:**
   - Remove the turkey and vegetable skewers from the grill or oven.
   - Serve immediately, garnished with fresh herbs if desired.

Tips:

- **Vegetable Variations:** Feel free to use other vegetables such as mushrooms, squash, or cherry tomatoes.
- **Grilling Tips:** Make sure the grill is well-heated before adding the skewers to ensure even cooking and nice grill marks.
- **Serving Suggestions:** Serve the turkey and vegetable skewers with a side of rice, quinoa, or a fresh salad for a complete meal.

These turkey and vegetable skewers are not only flavorful and satisfying but also a great way to incorporate lean protein and vegetables into your meal. Enjoy these skewers as a healthy and delicious option for lunch or dinner!

Roasted Cauliflower Steaks

Ingredients:

- 1 large head of cauliflower
- 3-4 tablespoons olive oil
- 2-3 cloves garlic, minced
- 1 teaspoon paprika
- 1/2 teaspoon ground cumin
- 1/2 teaspoon ground coriander
- Salt and pepper, to taste
- Fresh herbs (such as parsley or thyme), chopped, for garnish
- Lemon wedges, for serving (optional)

Instructions:

1. **Preheat the Oven:**
   - Preheat your oven to 425°F (220°C). Line a baking sheet with parchment paper or foil for easy cleanup.
2. **Prepare the Cauliflower:**
   - Remove the leaves from the cauliflower and trim the stem end, making sure the cauliflower stands flat on a cutting board.
   - Cut the cauliflower into 1-inch thick slices. These slices will be your cauliflower steaks.
3. **Season the Cauliflower Steaks:**
   - In a small bowl, whisk together olive oil, minced garlic, paprika, ground cumin, ground coriander, salt, and pepper.
   - Brush both sides of each cauliflower steak with the seasoned olive oil mixture, ensuring they are well coated.
4. **Roast the Cauliflower Steaks:**
   - Place the cauliflower steaks on the prepared baking sheet in a single layer.
   - Roast in the preheated oven for 25-30 minutes, flipping halfway through, or until the cauliflower is tender and golden brown on the edges.
5. **Serve:**
   - Transfer the roasted cauliflower steaks to a serving platter.
   - Garnish with freshly chopped herbs, such as parsley or thyme.
   - Serve hot with lemon wedges on the side for squeezing over the steaks, if desired.

Tips:

- **Uniform Slices:** Try to cut the cauliflower into even slices to ensure even cooking.
- **Seasoning Variations:** Feel free to customize the seasoning blend with your favorite herbs and spices, such as smoked paprika, chili flakes, or curry powder.

- **Serving Suggestions:** Serve the roasted cauliflower steaks with a side of quinoa, couscous, or a fresh green salad for a complete meal.

Roasted cauliflower steaks are a delicious and versatile dish that highlights the natural sweetness and nuttiness of cauliflower. They make a satisfying vegetarian option that's easy to prepare and full of flavor!

Mixed Berry Smoothie Bowl

Ingredients:

- 1 cup mixed berries (such as strawberries, blueberries, raspberries, blackberries)
- 1 ripe banana, frozen
- 1/2 cup plain Greek yogurt
- 1/4 cup almond milk (or any milk of your choice)
- 1 tablespoon honey or maple syrup (optional, for sweetness)
- Toppings (optional):
  - Fresh berries (sliced strawberries, blueberries, raspberries)
  - Granola
  - Chia seeds
  - Sliced almonds or other nuts
  - Coconut flakes
  - Fresh mint leaves

Instructions:

1. **Prepare the Smoothie Base:**
   - In a blender, combine mixed berries, frozen banana, Greek yogurt, almond milk, and honey or maple syrup (if using). Blend until smooth and creamy. Add more almond milk if needed to reach your desired consistency.
2. **Assemble the Smoothie Bowl:**
   - Pour the mixed berry smoothie into a bowl.
3. **Add Toppings:**
   - Arrange your desired toppings on top of the smoothie bowl. You can create a decorative pattern or simply sprinkle them over the top.
4. **Serve:**
   - Enjoy your mixed berry smoothie bowl immediately with a spoon.

Tips:

- **Frozen Fruit:** Using a frozen banana helps create a thick and creamy texture for the smoothie bowl.
- **Customize Toppings:** Feel free to customize the toppings based on your preferences and what you have on hand. You can also add other fruits, nuts, seeds, or even a drizzle of nut butter.
- **Nutritional Boost:** Consider adding protein powder or a spoonful of ground flaxseed for an extra nutritional boost.

Smoothie bowls are not only delicious but also versatile and can be tailored to suit different tastes and dietary preferences. They are a great way to start your day with a nutritious and satisfying meal!

Mediterranean Grilled Chicken

Ingredients:

- 4 boneless, skinless chicken breasts
- 1/4 cup extra virgin olive oil
- 3 cloves garlic, minced
- 1 teaspoon dried oregano
- 1 teaspoon dried basil
- 1 teaspoon dried thyme
- 1/2 teaspoon paprika
- 1/2 teaspoon ground cumin
- Salt and pepper, to taste
- Juice of 1 lemon
- Fresh parsley or cilantro, chopped, for garnish
- Lemon wedges, for serving (optional)

Instructions:

1. **Prepare the Marinade:**
    - In a small bowl, whisk together olive oil, minced garlic, dried oregano, dried basil, dried thyme, paprika, ground cumin, salt, pepper, and lemon juice.
2. **Marinate the Chicken:**
    - Place the chicken breasts in a shallow dish or a large resealable plastic bag. Pour the marinade over the chicken, making sure each piece is coated evenly. Marinate in the refrigerator for at least 30 minutes, or up to 4 hours for maximum flavor.
3. **Preheat the Grill:**
    - Preheat your grill to medium-high heat.
4. **Grill the Chicken:**
    - Remove the chicken breasts from the marinade, shaking off any excess.
    - Grill the chicken breasts for about 6-7 minutes per side, or until they are cooked through and reach an internal temperature of 165°F (75°C). Cooking time may vary depending on the thickness of the chicken breasts.
5. **Rest and Serve:**
    - Remove the grilled chicken from the grill and let it rest for a few minutes before serving.
    - Garnish with freshly chopped parsley or cilantro.
6. **Serve:**
    - Serve the Mediterranean grilled chicken hot, accompanied by your favorite sides such as rice, quinoa, or a fresh salad.

Tips:

- **Variations:** You can add a pinch of red pepper flakes for a hint of spice or substitute fresh herbs for dried herbs if available.
- **Serving Suggestions:** Mediterranean grilled chicken pairs well with tzatziki sauce, hummus, or a side of grilled vegetables.
- **Leftovers:** Leftover grilled chicken can be stored in an airtight container in the refrigerator for up to 3-4 days and used in salads, wraps, or sandwiches.

This Mediterranean grilled chicken recipe is perfect for a healthy and flavorful meal that captures the essence of Mediterranean cuisine. Enjoy the juicy and herb-infused chicken with your favorite Mediterranean-inspired sides!

Ratatouille with Eggplant and Zucchini

Ingredients:

- 1 large eggplant, cut into 1-inch cubes
- 2 medium zucchini, sliced into rounds or half-moons
- 1 red bell pepper, sliced
- 1 yellow bell pepper, sliced
- 1 onion, thinly sliced
- 3 cloves garlic, minced
- 2 cups diced tomatoes (fresh or canned)
- 2 tablespoons tomato paste
- 1 teaspoon dried thyme (or 1 tablespoon fresh thyme leaves)
- 1 teaspoon dried oregano
- Salt and pepper, to taste
- 3 tablespoons olive oil
- Fresh basil leaves, chopped, for garnish

Instructions:

1. **Prepare the Vegetables:**
   - Heat 2 tablespoons of olive oil in a large skillet or Dutch oven over medium heat. Add the sliced onion and sauté for 3-4 minutes until softened.
   - Add minced garlic to the skillet and cook for another 1-2 minutes until fragrant.
2. **Cook the Vegetables:**
   - Add the cubed eggplant, sliced zucchini, and sliced bell peppers to the skillet. Season with salt, pepper, dried thyme, and dried oregano. Stir well to combine.
   - Cook the vegetables for about 8-10 minutes, stirring occasionally, until they start to soften.
3. **Add Tomatoes and Tomato Paste:**
   - Stir in the diced tomatoes (with their juices) and tomato paste. Mix everything together until well combined.
4. **Simmer:**
   - Reduce the heat to low, cover the skillet or Dutch oven, and let the ratatouille simmer gently for 20-25 minutes, or until all the vegetables are tender and flavors have melded together. Stir occasionally to prevent sticking.
5. **Adjust Seasoning and Serve:**
   - Taste and adjust the seasoning with salt and pepper as needed.
6. **Garnish and Serve:**
   - Remove the ratatouille from heat. Garnish with chopped fresh basil leaves.
   - Serve hot, warm, or at room temperature as a main dish or side dish. Ratatouille pairs well with crusty bread, rice, quinoa, or pasta.

Tips:

- **Vegetable Consistency:** Try to cut the vegetables into similar-sized pieces for even cooking.
- **Variations:** Ratatouille is versatile, so feel free to add other vegetables such as mushrooms or carrots, or adjust the herbs and spices according to your taste.
- **Storage:** Ratatouille tastes even better the next day as the flavors continue to meld. Store leftovers in an airtight container in the refrigerator for up to 3-4 days.

This ratatouille with eggplant and zucchini recipe is a delicious and hearty dish that celebrates the flavors of fresh vegetables and Mediterranean cuisine. Enjoy this comforting and nutritious stew any time of the year!

Baked Sweet Potato Fries

Ingredients:

- 2 large sweet potatoes, peeled (optional) and cut into thin strips
- 2 tablespoons olive oil
- 1 teaspoon paprika
- 1/2 teaspoon garlic powder
- 1/2 teaspoon onion powder
- 1/2 teaspoon dried thyme (optional)
- Salt and pepper, to taste
- Optional: 1-2 tablespoons cornstarch (for extra crispiness)

Instructions:

1. **Preheat the Oven:**
   - Preheat your oven to 425°F (220°C). Line a baking sheet with parchment paper or aluminum foil for easy cleanup.
2. **Prepare the Sweet Potatoes:**
   - Peel the sweet potatoes (if desired) and cut them into thin, uniform strips to ensure even cooking.
3. **Coat with Seasonings:**
   - In a large bowl, toss the sweet potato strips with olive oil, paprika, garlic powder, onion powder, dried thyme (if using), salt, and pepper. For extra crispiness, you can toss the sweet potato strips with cornstarch before adding the seasonings.
4. **Arrange on Baking Sheet:**
   - Spread the sweet potato strips in a single layer on the prepared baking sheet, making sure they are not overcrowded. This allows them to crisp up evenly.
5. **Bake:**
   - Bake in the preheated oven for 20-25 minutes, flipping halfway through, or until the sweet potato fries are crispy and golden brown.
6. **Serve:**
   - Remove from the oven and let the sweet potato fries cool slightly on the baking sheet.
   - Serve hot, optionally with a sprinkle of additional salt or your favorite dipping sauce (such as ketchup, aioli, or ranch dressing).

Tips:

- **Uniform Size:** Cut the sweet potato strips into similar sizes to ensure they cook evenly.
- **Crispy Tip:** Soaking the cut sweet potatoes in cold water for about 30 minutes before patting them dry and seasoning can help remove excess starch and make them crispier.
- **Variations:** Feel free to customize the seasonings with your favorite herbs and spices, such as smoked paprika, cayenne pepper for heat, or a sprinkle of Parmesan cheese.

These baked sweet potato fries are a healthier alternative to fried potatoes and make a delicious side dish or snack. Enjoy their crispy exterior and sweet flavor guilt-free!

Whole Grain Couscous Salad

Ingredients:

- 1 cup whole grain couscous
- 1 1/4 cups water or vegetable broth
- 1 cup cherry tomatoes, halved
- 1 cucumber, diced
- 1/2 red bell pepper, diced
- 1/2 yellow bell pepper, diced
- 1/4 cup red onion, finely chopped
- 1/4 cup fresh parsley, chopped
- 1/4 cup fresh mint leaves, chopped
- 1/4 cup Kalamata olives, pitted and halved (optional)
- 1/4 cup crumbled feta cheese (optional)
- Juice of 1 lemon
- 3 tablespoons extra virgin olive oil
- 1 clove garlic, minced
- 1/2 teaspoon dried oregano
- Salt and pepper, to taste

Instructions:

1. **Cook the Whole Grain Couscous:**
    - In a medium saucepan, bring water or vegetable broth to a boil.
    - Stir in whole grain couscous. Cover the saucepan, remove from heat, and let it sit for 5 minutes. Fluff the couscous with a fork to separate the grains.
2. **Prepare the Dressing:**
    - In a small bowl, whisk together lemon juice, extra virgin olive oil, minced garlic, dried oregano, salt, and pepper to make the dressing.
3. **Assemble the Salad:**
    - In a large bowl, combine cooked whole grain couscous with cherry tomatoes, cucumber, red bell pepper, yellow bell pepper, red onion, parsley, mint leaves, and Kalamata olives (if using).
4. **Add the Dressing:**
    - Pour the dressing over the couscous salad ingredients. Toss gently to coat everything evenly with the dressing.
5. **Optional: Add Feta Cheese:**
    - If using, sprinkle crumbled feta cheese over the couscous salad and toss gently to combine.
6. **Chill and Serve:**
    - Cover the bowl with plastic wrap and refrigerate for at least 30 minutes to allow the flavors to meld together.

- Serve the whole grain couscous salad chilled or at room temperature. It can be enjoyed as a side dish or a light main course.

Tips:

- **Variations:** Feel free to add other vegetables such as diced avocado, grated carrots, or roasted vegetables to the couscous salad.
- **Make Ahead:** This salad can be made ahead of time and stored in the refrigerator for up to 2-3 days. Add fresh herbs just before serving to keep them vibrant.
- **Protein Boost:** For a heartier salad, add grilled chicken, chickpeas, or tofu cubes.

This whole grain couscous salad is not only delicious and colorful but also packed with nutrients and fiber. It's perfect for picnics, potlucks, or as a wholesome lunch option!

Chicken and Vegetable Kebabs

Ingredients:

- 1 pound boneless, skinless chicken breasts or thighs, cut into 1-inch cubes
- 1 red bell pepper, cut into chunks
- 1 yellow bell pepper, cut into chunks
- 1 red onion, cut into chunks
- 1 zucchini, sliced into rounds
- 8-10 cherry tomatoes
- Wooden or metal skewers

Marinade:

- 1/4 cup olive oil
- 2 cloves garlic, minced
- 1 teaspoon dried oregano
- 1 teaspoon dried thyme
- 1 teaspoon paprika
- Juice of 1 lemon
- Salt and pepper, to taste

Instructions:

1. **Prepare the Marinade:**
   - In a small bowl, whisk together olive oil, minced garlic, dried oregano, dried thyme, paprika, lemon juice, salt, and pepper.
2. **Marinate the Chicken:**
   - Place the chicken cubes in a shallow dish or a large resealable plastic bag. Pour the marinade over the chicken, making sure each piece is coated evenly. Marinate in the refrigerator for at least 30 minutes, or up to 2 hours for maximum flavor.
3. **Prepare the Vegetables:**
   - While the chicken is marinating, prepare the vegetables by cutting them into chunks or slices.
4. **Assemble the Kebabs:**
   - If using wooden skewers, soak them in water for at least 30 minutes to prevent them from burning during cooking.
   - Thread the marinated chicken cubes and prepared vegetables onto the skewers, alternating between chicken, bell peppers, onion, zucchini, and cherry tomatoes.
5. **Grill or Bake:**
   - Preheat your grill to medium-high heat or preheat your oven to 400°F (200°C).

- Grill the kebabs over medium-high heat for about 10-12 minutes, turning occasionally, or until the chicken is cooked through and the vegetables are tender and lightly charred.
- If baking, place the skewers on a baking sheet lined with parchment paper or aluminum foil. Bake for 15-20 minutes, or until the chicken is cooked through and the vegetables are tender.

6. **Serve:**
   - Remove the chicken and vegetable kebabs from the grill or oven.
   - Serve hot, optionally garnished with fresh herbs like parsley or cilantro.

Tips:

- **Vegetable Variations:** Feel free to use other vegetables such as mushrooms, cherry tomatoes, or chunks of squash.
- **Serving Suggestions:** Serve the chicken and vegetable kebabs with rice, couscous, or a fresh salad. They also pair well with tzatziki sauce or a squeeze of lemon juice.
- **Leftovers:** Leftover kebabs can be stored in an airtight container in the refrigerator for up to 3-4 days and reheated for a quick and delicious meal.

These chicken and vegetable kebabs are not only easy to make but also a healthy and colorful dish that's perfect for outdoor grilling or indoor baking. Enjoy the combination of juicy chicken and tender vegetables with your favorite sides!

Beet and Quinoa Salad

Ingredients:

- 1 cup quinoa, rinsed
- 2 cups water or vegetable broth
- 3 medium beets, roasted or boiled, peeled, and diced
- 1/2 cup crumbled feta cheese (optional)
- 1/4 cup chopped fresh parsley or cilantro
- 1/4 cup chopped walnuts or pecans (optional)
- 1/4 cup dried cranberries or raisins (optional)
- Juice of 1 lemon
- 3 tablespoons extra virgin olive oil
- 1 tablespoon balsamic vinegar
- Salt and pepper, to taste

Instructions:

1. **Cook the Quinoa:**
   - In a medium saucepan, combine quinoa and water or vegetable broth. Bring to a boil over medium-high heat.
   - Reduce the heat to low, cover, and simmer for 15-20 minutes, or until the quinoa is cooked and the liquid is absorbed. Remove from heat and let it cool slightly.
2. **Prepare the Dressing:**
   - In a small bowl, whisk together lemon juice, extra virgin olive oil, balsamic vinegar, salt, and pepper to make the dressing.
3. **Assemble the Salad:**
   - In a large bowl, combine cooked quinoa, diced roasted or boiled beets, crumbled feta cheese (if using), chopped fresh parsley or cilantro, chopped nuts (if using), and dried cranberries or raisins (if using).
4. **Add the Dressing:**
   - Pour the dressing over the salad ingredients. Toss gently to coat everything evenly with the dressing.
5. **Chill and Serve:**
   - Cover the bowl with plastic wrap and refrigerate for at least 30 minutes to allow the flavors to meld together.
   - Serve the beet and quinoa salad chilled or at room temperature. It can be enjoyed as a side dish or a light main course.

Tips:

- **Roasting Beets:** To roast beets, wrap them individually in aluminum foil and bake in a preheated oven at 400°F (200°C) for about 45-60 minutes, or until tender when pierced with a fork.

- **Variations:** Feel free to customize the salad with additional vegetables like spinach or arugula, or add avocado slices for creaminess.
- **Make Ahead:** This salad can be made ahead of time and stored in the refrigerator for up to 3-4 days. Add fresh herbs just before serving to keep them vibrant.

This beet and quinoa salad is not only delicious and colorful but also packed with fiber, vitamins, and minerals. Enjoy its refreshing flavors and nutritious benefits as a wholesome addition to your meals!

www.ingramcontent.com/pod-product-compliance
Lightning Source LLC
LaVergne TN
LVHW081602060526
838201LV00054B/2035